SCREENING IMAGES:

IDEAS FOR MEDIA EDUCATION

CHRIS M. WORSNOP

Wright Communications, Mississauga, Canada

© 1999 Chris M. Worsnop

Published by
Wright Communications
2400 Dundas Street West
Unit 6, Suite 107
Mississauga, Ontario
L5K 1H9

Canadian Cataloguing in Publication Data

Worsnop, Chris M.
  Screening Images: ideas for media education

2nd ed.
ISBN 0-9697954-2-4

  1. Mass media—Study and teaching. I. Title.

LB1028.4.W67 1999   302.23'07   C99-900564-2

Cover design by Neil Bruce
Printed and bound in Canada
9 8 7 6 5 4 3 2

This Book is dedicated to the Memory of
MARGARET BRITT

Margaret Britt served for more than thirty years as a film information officer with the Canadian Film Institute (CFI) and National Archives in Ottawa. She died of cancer in 1986. I first met her in 1965 when I was trying to get some film study into my English curriculum in an Ottawa secondary school. She was then working at the (CFI) as the film officer; as soon as she heard what I was trying to do, she made it her business to give me access to as much of the CFI collection as possible. She was constantly suggesting titles to me and putting me in touch with other film teachers.

Later, when I moved from Ottawa, it was Margaret who got me involved in the **Film Federation of Eastern Ontario,** *who introduced me to the then new* **Ontario Film Association** *(now,* **the Association for the Advancement of Visual Media/l'association pour l'avancement des medias visuels)** *Annual Film Showcase, and who eventually nominated me for the board of that organization.*

Margaret was the editor of the OFA publication, **A Newsletter Called Fred** *(now,* **Visual Media/medias visuels),** *and in no time at all she had me writing for it. She was an encyclopedia of film information, an indefatigable worker. Even in the very worst of adversity, her cheerfulness and optimism was infectious. She was a great person to have as a friend.*

When she died, OFA, recognizing the magnitude of her contribution to the non-theatrical film world in Canada, established an annual scholarship in her name. I was honored to receive one of those scholarships to help in the writing of this book, and I am equally honored to dedicate the book to Margaret Britt, my long time mentor and friend in the film world, and one who is to a large extent responsible for my continued interest in both media education and writing.

Margaret, we miss you, but we'll never forget.
CMW, January, 1994, July, 1999

ACKNOWLEDGEMENTS

Nobody ever writes a book without the help of many people, and I wish to acknowledge all that help with sincere thanks.

First, to the Association for the Advancement of Visual Media/ l'association pour l'avancement des medias visuels, for their encouragement to go on with the project, for their support for my column, Screening Images *in their periodical,* Visual Media/medias visuels, *and for their granting me the Margaret Britt Memorial Scholarship.*

Next, to my family who have responded to my constant need to be writing with understanding, encouragement and love. It's really hard to keep going without any of those, and I have always been blessed with an abundance of all of them from my wife, Brenda, and from my children.

I particularly want to thank my daughter, Jennifer, as well as her older brother, Matthew who over a number of years have provided topics for many of the chapters in Part 2.

Brenda, too, has made a very significant contribution to the book, through her expert knowledge and tutoring in word processing and desk-top publishing.

I wish to thank also all the people who, hearing that the first edition was going out of print, persuaded me to go ahead with this second edition.

TABLE OF CONTENTS

PART THREE:
IDEAS FOR MEDIA EDUCATION ACTIVITIES

APPENDIX:

PREFACE TO THE SECOND EDITION

When supplies of the first edition of *Screening Images* began to dwindle, I had to decide if I should reprint the first edition, write a new book altogether, or put out a second edition. I talked to a lot of people as I struggled with this decision, and in the end they convinced me that the content of the first edition was not out of date, and should remain available to people interested in media education.

Readers who know the first edition will recognize that the second edition is different in a number of ways:

- Many of the references have been updated
- There are several chapters of new material, mostly in Part 2 (Look for the chapter headings with line-borders)
- The activities in Part 3 have been numbered for ease of reference
- The black-line masters have been moved into another publication - *Assessing Media Work: Authentic Assessment in Media Education*, (Wright Communications, 1996)

One of the most important things you can know about this book is that it is not intended to be read like a novel. It didn't get written all at once, and it is not intended to be read that way. Feel free to hop, skip and jump among the chapters and sections to make the book serve your own purposes. You may want to skip the theoretical bits at the beginning and go straight to the more practical sections; you may decide to ignore the suggestions for classroom activities; it doesn't matter, as long as you can find some use and help within these pages for your own needs in media education.

INTRODUCTION

WHAT MEDIA EDUCATION IS LIKE

Much of what you are about to read in this book is based on the premise that teaching the media is not a mystery confined only to a certain erudite set of cognoscenti, but something that any good teacher like you can readily handle in class using your existing knowledge and expertise.

The expertise will come from your experience as a teacher, and from your experience with the media. You already know a lot about helping youngsters learn, and helping youngsters learn media is easier than in many other subjects, because the subject matter is something that the kids already like. We just have to be careful not to ruin it for them by turning it into another turgid school "subject" full of stuff that we know and the students have to learn. (I have never forgotten the young man in my grade 13 class in Ottawa who reacted to my announcement of the first film course in the school by saying, "You're not going to do the same thing to films that you did to books, are you?" I have never forgotten the moment, and I have always tried to heed the admonition.)

Being nervous about teaching in a new subject area is rather like being nervous about swimming in deep water. Even when we know already how to swim, we hesitate to venture into new water, especially if it is deep. There's wisdom in this: caution is always to be recommended. But still, most swimmers realize that they swim only in the top metre of the water, and that all the water below need not be a threat. Knowing something about the water is certainly an advantage to any swimmer, but we all know also that the depth of the water does not diminish our competence as swimmers. Teaching is very much the same: once we know how to be good teachers, we have mastered the top metre of our professional pool, and we needn't feel threatened by the rest.

All that you already know about independent and group learning will serve you very well in the media classroom; any courses or workshops you have taken on learning styles or the process of learning will be useful in the media class; all those hours you have spent at the cinema, in front of the TV, listening to radio or recorded music, or reading newspapers and magazines will suddenly be turned into research time for one of the most important study areas in modern curriculum.

I've been an Ontario English teacher for the almost 40 years, spending 25 of those years as an English co-ordinator. I've learned a lot about curriculum in reading and writing in those years. It has only been very recently, though, that I've begun to understand that the insights I've developed as an English teacher and co-ordinator are the same ones I need as a teacher of media. Nearly everything I know about reading, and writing, and responding, and process in English curriculum is applicable to the teaching of media.

The same is true for you. What you already know about teaching is applicable to your teaching of media. You don't have to be nervous about media being a new specialty that you need to study before you attempt anything in your classroom. Let media be an exploration for you and for your students. Have the nerve to learn about it together - to make it a true discovery process. Be prepared to say, "I don't know. How could we find out?" The truth, most likely, is that you do know, but that you weren't aware that you knew, rather like Molliere's Bourgeois Gentilhomme, M. Jourdain, who discovered in his middle age that he'd been speaking prose all his life.

A great deal of what we know about the media is informal knowledge: stuff that we learned as we took part in the media. We know, without knowing how we know, when a program on TV is coming to an end, who are the good and the bad guys in movies, what certain kinds of music are supposed to mean on a soundtrack, or which newspapers our neighbors would subscribe to. Media education is the process of bringing that natural knowledge into the forefront of our consciousness so that it can be examined and refined.

Some people, people who have made a life-time study or a career of the media, have developed a specialty vocabulary to describe their knowledge - a jargon. You shouldn't feel threatened by this jargon, and you should avoid making the learning of it too important for either yourself or for your students. When you begin to develop new concepts about things, you'll find that you need names for those concepts, and the jargon will begin to make sense to you. One of the silliest things that you or your students could do is try to memorize lists of media terminology in the belief that you were learning about media by doing so.

Media education is a quest for meaning. Much of the value of a quest lies in the search itself as well as in the achievement of the goal.

I do not intend to say that you never need to do anything in your media class other than sit back and wait for miracles to happen. As an interested teacher, you should be ready to do some reading about media education, to attend some workshops and conferences, and, eventually, to take some courses. Ignorance need not be a hindrance to getting started, but it is not a state you should actively protect. But I do not need to tell you this. If you did not already know it to be true, you would not be reading this book. You are already one of those competent swimmers who is learning snorkelling and scuba diving to find out more about the rest of the water.

MEDIA STUDY, MEDIA EDUCATION OR MEDIA LITERACY?

Media teachers today use the terms "media education", "media study", and "media literacy" almost interchangeably. My personal preference is to use the term "media education" as a broad description of all that takes place in a media-oriented classroom, whether the subject matter is English, history, geography or science. There's plenty of media learning that can be done in all of those subject areas and others. Where schools or teachers organize separate courses or units specifically to study the media, then I would use the term "media study" to describe that kind of work. "Media literacy" is the outcome of work in either media education or media study. The more you learn about or through the media, the more media literacy you have: media literacy is the skills of experiencing, interpreting/analyzing and making media products.

Examples of other terminology that you might come across are: "film studies", "film criticism", and "screen education". Film studies is a term often used in colleges and universities to describe courses that treat film as a formal discipline, like literature. Film studies courses would cover material like theories of film and of film criticism; the work of certain film "greats"; the history of film. Film criticism courses would be similar, but would concentrate on reading the work of film critics and on learning the skills and conventions of writing criticism. Screen education is a term that describes an approach very similar to media education as we practice it now, but restricted to the study of the screen media: film, TV, photography, and more recently, computer-based media.

One other term that is beginning to be heard more frequently now is, "cultural studies". It is used to describe an expanding area of university study embracing all aspects of culture, and drawing upon a blend of linguistic, critical, political and sociological approaches.

I'd like to establish one other term. I will be referring

throughout this book to "media texts", meaning any piece of media that we encounter. A mass produced T-shirt is a media text, as is a popular song, a TV program, a newspaper advertisement, a piece of junk mail or a feature film extract. Any piece of expression within a medium is a text.

SCREENING IMAGES

PART ONE

IDEAS ABOUT

EDUCATION

(AND MEDIA)

READING,

DECONSTRUCTION,

MOTORCYCLES AND

MEDIA EDUCATION

What you already know about reading in language arts is very largely applicable in media education. Reading and learning theories implemented by teachers in their reading and literature programs can be applied with little modification in a media education class. Here are three basic ideas about reading theory that have influenced my understanding of media education in recent years:

- decoding is not reading
- comprehension depends to a large extent on what you already know
- reading, like nearly every other human activity, is part of the task of making sense out of the world.

DECODING IS NOT READING

The first of these ideas points out the difference between decoding and recoding in the reading process. Decoding is the process of taking coded language, (print) and removing the print code so that the message can again be rendered into words. Some people think that reading consists of nothing more: decoding print to words.

However, if you understand that the author began not with words but with meaning, and that the meaning was put into words before the words were put into print, then it should be obvious that the job of the reader is not merely to get back from the code of print to

3

the words, but to get back from the words to the meaning. This part of the reading process can be called "re-coding into meaning". Readers who merely decode from print to words have been described as doing nothing more than "barking at print", or "shouting out the names of the words".

The process of reading can be described in a diagram like this.

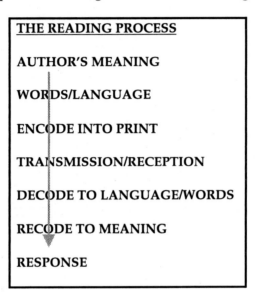

THE READING PROCESS

AUTHOR'S MEANING

WORDS/LANGUAGE

ENCODE INTO PRINT

TRANSMISSION/RECEPTION

DECODE TO LANGUAGE/WORDS

RECODE TO MEANING

RESPONSE

COMPREHENSION DEPENDS ON WHAT YOU ALREADY KNOW

The second idea from reading theory is the notion that our ability to comprehend - to make meaning - depends as much on what we already know as on what we can take from the text. For instance, you would find it difficult to read a text about nuclear physics, no matter how simply it was written, unless you already knew something about the subject. For example, try making sense out of the following passage. I'll even give you a clue: It's about the game of cricket. Yet I'll almost guarantee that unless you already know something about cricket, the text will make remarkably little sense to you. By the way, it measures out at between the grade 5 and 7 levels of difficulty on a number of different readability scales.

Hammond came striding out of the pavilion towards the wicket. His side was 183 for 7 and needed another eighty to avoid the follow-on. As he approached mid off, he paused to tuck in the strap on his leg.. pad. Then he continued towards the pitch. When he reached the crease, he took a careful guard, marked middle and leg.., checking it twice with the umpire. He then surveyed the field, adjusted his cap and took his stance.

Stevenedge at the other end began his run. Seven, eight, nine strides and then, his back leg.. trailing, he brought his left arm over, snapping the ball as it left his hand. It was a full pitch with a wicked spin on it. Hammond wisely went out and stone-walled it before it could bite into the turf.

That was the last ball of the over, another wicket maiden for Stevenedge.

148 words. Readability grade 5-7

The amount of sense you were able to make out of this text on cricket, (let's use Frank Smith's term, "visual information" as a synonym for text) depends to a large extent on how much information you were able to bring to it from your own internal banks of knowledge, memory and experience. (Smith calls these personal banks of experience "non-visual information".) If you already have plenty of non-visual information about cricket, then you can explain that a "wicket maiden" is a series of six balls ("pitches", to North Americans) in which no runs have been scored and one batter has been "out". You might also be able to explain the intricacies of meaning that reside in that common and tiny word, "leg.." in the expression "middle and leg..". Good luck!

SCREENING IMAGES

It doesn't really matter, except to illustrate that the amount of meaning a reader is able to take from a text depends to quite some extent on the information that the reader brings to it. Nuclear physics or cricket it's all the same, if you know nothing to begin with, you have a hard job of getting the meaning out of a new text. Media texts are similar to written texts. We approach them with our personal store of non-visual information and make as much of their visual (or aural, or other) information as we can.

Most media texts are really quite familiar to us. We already have a lot of non-visual information about media, and about the kinds of things that media tend to depict for us. We know just what to expect of our TV and radio and popular music and movies. They rarely surprise us, except, paradoxically, in predictable ways. Getting to the meaning of media texts can be very easy, because we have all spent hundreds and thousands of hours becoming familiar with the kinds of media messages that are available to us. We all learned the codes of media as naturally as we learned to talk, without having to go through the kind of artificial, alphabetic learning that most of us experienced in learning to read.

But one of the consequences of learning media codes naturally is that we tend to be quite uncritical about all the media messages we consume, and allow them to wash over us without giving them a second thought. "Giving a second thought" has a lot to do with what media education is all about. "Giving a second thought" is one of the most important skills of media literacy. Second thoughts often help us get to deeper, or hidden meanings, and can lead to better understanding both of the text and of ourselves. This is the source of critical thinking. (See **TAKING A SECOND LOOK**)

Suppose that in your approach to the text on cricket, you had been given the chance to talk in small groups about everything you knew about the game, before you read the text. Chances are that you would have remembered some detail you had previously forgotten, or someone would contribute some knowledge no-one else had, or someone would be a cricket expert. In any event, the experience of talking in the group would bring all of your group's accumulated non-visual information about cricket to the fore-front of your consciousness, making it much more ready for application to the visual information of the text. Warm-up activities like this are vital in all learning, including learning in media classrooms.

This brings us to the connection between media education and what literature teachers call "response theory".

NON-VISUAL INFORMATION AND RESPONSE THEORY

In modern language arts classrooms, response theory plays a very important role. Students react to a text, a poem or a novel, not according to some set of rules laid out by dusty theorists in some distant university or time, but according to their honest and detailed analysis of their personal response. You could say that a personal response is a reflection on the way that the visual and the non-visual information fit together. If a story makes a student laugh, then the student has to explain three things about the response:

1. what it was in the text that created the response. (What was funny in the story)
2. what it is in the student that connects with that text. (What experiences, hopes, fears, emotions, memories (non-visual information) are touched by the text)
3. the exact nature of the connection between the text and the reader's non-visual experience. (How the student explains the nature of the connection between the text and the self)

Naturally, individuals will have different responses to the same text, since no two of them have an identical set of non-visual experiences. Where one may laugh, it is entirely possible that another may cry. Both responses are valid. There is no question of right or wrong. The quality of the responses can be assessed by how well the students are able to explain them, and how clearly they can describe the connections between themselves and the text. Obviously response theory, an application of the concept of non-visual information, can be applied equally to media texts and to literary texts. It would be confusing for students if schools tried to do anything else.

READING, LIKE NEARLY EVERY OTHER HUMAN ACTIVITY, IS PART OF THE TASK OF MAKING SENSE OUT OF THE WORLD

In *Reading Without Nonsense* Frank Smith expanded on another simple and yet crucial concept of reading theory. It goes like this: the chief purposes in life is to make sense out of the world. One of the first jobs of life is to learn language. Infants undertake this job without much prompting, because it is obvious to them that language is the key to making sense of the world. After a very few years of life children realize they need to be able to read to get at a whole new section of information about the meaning of the world.

Making sense of the world is the larger idea of which making meaning from texts is only a part. The two ideas support each other and, together with the third idea about response theory, they help to explain my own philosophy of media education, and how media education is not so very different from a lot of other learning enterprises that we undertake in schools.

DECONSTRUCTION AND MOTOR-CYCLE MAINTENANCE

I used to have a neighbor whose pet possession was his motorcycle. Every year he would strip the machine down to its component parts, and lay them lovingly out on the driveway while he polished, oiled and adjusted each one. He eagerly explained how important it was for the motorcycle to receive this regular maintenance. However, it's important to notice that he always put the pieces back together again in order to make a motorcycle. The very purpose of taking it to pieces was to understand the motorcycle better, to be able to put it back together in better shape than before. If my neighbor had merely left the pieces around, shiny and well-oiled though they were, there would have been no doubt about his skills of deconstruction, but there also would have been no motorcycle to show for these skills. The purpose of deconstruction was to produce a better, or better understood motorcycle upon reconstruction. Reconstructing motorcycles can be very much like examining media texts.

PROCESS OF MOTORCYCLE MAINTENANCE	
MOTORCYCLE	
	--------------------DECONSTRUCT
MOTORCYCLE PARTS	
	------------MANIPULATE PARTS
SLIGHTLY DIFFERENT MOTORCYCLE	--------------------RECONSTRUCT

Ideas for Media Education

All texts are constructions, just as motorcycles are. They are deliberately put together by their authors who carefully arrange the different components to make up a text. While we may be used to saying that we saw an accident on the TV news, we realize that we did not see the accident itself, but only a representation of it, and that the representation may well show the accident in a different way from how it actually happened. Editing, camera work, and commentary are all components of TV news messages and are part of the construction process. In order to understand media messages best, we need to undo that construction, or "deconstruct" the messages. We need to strip it like a motorcycle.

Makers of media texts, just like writers, begin, not with the text itself, or even the component parts of it, but with concepts - meanings - which they intend to communicate. When we deconstruct a media text, or when we teach students how to do so, we are taking it apart to see how its components are put together. These components are not just concrete attributes like camera angles or musical effects, but they can also be abstractions such as mood, psychological purpose or ideology. When we deconstruct a media text, we're doing the same job as a reader who decodes print into words. And if we stop there, we are making a mistake about media education - a mistake just as fundamental as the one that decoders make about reading. The important part of deconstruction comes after the text has been taken apart, when the perceiver reconstructs the message into some sort of personal meaning, and combines the components of the text with personal experience to make meaning. This is exactly what a reader does after decoding a printed text to get meaning.

Deconstruction, then, though a necessary and useful skill or set of skills in media literacy, in itself is not enough, just as knowledge of the rules of phonics is not enough to the person who can read out loud with accuracy, but who has no comprehension afterwards. Both sets of skills on their own could be described as "necessary, but not sufficient".

The job of the media observer is to make sense out of each part of the world, including media texts. Making sense means consciously pushing the process of media perception to the point of finding or making meaning.

Consider a second example. You come across a completed jig-saw puzzle on the floor of your child's bedroom, and, in a fury of tidiness, take it apart and put it away in its box. The next day, you find the same puzzle completed again in the same spot on the floor. How does your personal version of making sense of the world differ from the child's? Which one of you is more concerned about making sense out of bedrooms? Which one about making sense out of jig-saws? How do both views support the notion that what has been deconstructed needs to be reconstructed before it is "good"?

The concept of construction is very important in learning theory, for learning is not something which can be given from one person to another but, rather, something which the learner has to construct from the pieces gathered. Human learning is an act of construction that follows the pattern of data gathering, pattern recognition, generalization, hypothesizing, hypothesis testing and concept formation. Scientists refer to this process as " the scientific process".

So, in summary, we have deconstruction, reconstruction and construction. They work together like this: whenever we perceive a text, in media, print or just a text in life, we use our deconstruction skills to look at its parts and to understand how it was put together. This gives us motorcycle parts or jig-saw pieces. But because of our drive to make sense out of the world, we push beyond deconstruction to reconstruction. This gives us motorcycles and completed jig-saw puzzles instead of just pieces. Then we combine the meaning that we find in the text with our own store of human experience to integrate this new bit of meaning into our whole view of the world.

Since the making of meaning is such a personal process, and since each individual store of human experience is unique, there is little wonder that people respond differently to a common text. It is clear, too, that any theory of perception or of textual criticism based on the assumption that each individual text contains in itself somewhere a single correct interpretation is one which does not take the variety of human experience into account. Such theories are the antithesis of response theory, and deny students their individuality.

I am reminded here of the story of the Yorkshireman who was hit by a car at a stop light because of his dialectical interpretation of the warning text, "DO NOT CROSS WHILE THE LIGHT IS RED". For all that his response to the text was unfortunate, and almost certainly contrary to the intended meaning, the Yorkshireman never did concede that he was in any way in error, but criticized the message instead.

By the way, please do not interpret any bias into this example. Since I am myself both male and from Yorkshire, it is a tale that I consciously tell against myself.

PROCESS OF INTERPRETING A RED TRAFFIC LIGHT

MEANING---------	DANGER = RED
CODING -----------	"DO NOT CROSS WHILE THE LIGHT IS RED"
TRANSMISSION--	ILLUMINATED PRINTED LANGUAGE
DECODING -------	"DO NOT CROSS WHILE THE LIGHT IS RED"
RECODING -------	A: MOST DIALECTS, WHILE = WHEN B: YORKSHIRE DIALECT, WHILE = UNTIL
RESPONSE -------	A: STAND STILL UNTIL THE LIGHT CHANGES FROM RED B: WAIT FOR RED LIGHT, THEN CROSS

As a child in WW II England, I was conditioned to fear the sound of a rising and falling siren. When I was a young adult teaching in a small western Ontario town, the sound of the siren used to summon the volunteer fire brigade to duty meant to me something entirely different from what it meant to most other members of that community. The media message was the same. The intention of the message was unchanged. People's deconstruction of these messages was probably very similar, and yet the reconstruction and interpretation was drastically different because of differences in people's backgrounds.

Here is a diagram representing this piece of response.

SCREENING IMAGES

PROCESS OF INTERPRETING SIRENS

MEANING --------------	NEED TO SUMMON FIRE BRIGADE
CODING ------------------	CODED INTO SOUND OF SIREN
TRANSMISSION ------	SIREN SOUND/ AIR WAVES
DECODING ------------	RECOGNIZE A CERTAIN KIND OF SIREN
RECODING -------------	INTERPRET SIREN WITH PERSONAL EXPERIENCE
RESPONSE --------------	A. NEED FOR FIRE BRIGADE TO ASSEMBLE: DO NOTHING UNLESS YOU ARE A MEMBER OF THE FIRE BRIGADE
	B. PRESENCE OF ENEMY BOMBERS: TAKE COVER

Response theory now drives literature programs in our schools. And, surely, it only makes sense that we should connect our students' interpretations of non-print texts to the kind of theory of interpretation they use in their literature classrooms. It makes sense not only because we ought not to give students conflicting experiences and messages in schools, but also because the theory itself is valid and worthwhile.

And so we have a model for text perception. It begins with the making of the original text, or construction, (encoding in reading theory); moves on to the exploration of the text by a receiver through deconstruction, (decoding); proceeds to the stage of reconstruction to reconstitute a whole from the deconstructed parts, (recoding); and ends again with construction - the receiver builds a meaning out of the mixture of the perceived text and personal, non-visual information. What the sender constructs is a text. What the receiver constructs is meaning. Meanings, like texts, have to be put together.

All learning is construction. Everything we know, we have constructed for ourselves from components that came both from within us and from outside sources. There is no way of making knowledge except through this kind of construction. Information that we have merely memorized, without building it into a system of understanding, isn't much use to us. For students to learn, they have to be presented with chances to build meanings and to construct their own understandings of the world. Being told is rarely enough.

PROCESS OF MEDIA PERCEPTION		
	MEANING	
SKILLS AND TOOLS FOR MAKING MEDIA	CODING TRANSMISSION	_CONSTRUCTION
SKILLS AND TOOLS FOR EXAMINING MEDIA	RECEPTION DECODING RECODING RESPONSE	_DECONSTRUCTION _RECONSTRUCTION _CONSTRUCTION

My neighbor, though, didn't use just response theory in stripping and rebuilding his motorcycle. He also needed some tools, some skills and a certain working knowledge of motorcycles. When I asked him how he developed these skills and working knowledge, his answer was: "Fooling around with motorcycles." He picked up the tools, it seems as he found he absolutely needed them, or could afford them, or both. These messages of his are important for teachers of media.

    1.   You learn a lot from fooling around.
    2.   You don't need the tools until you need them.
        a)   If you can't afford the tools, you find another way of doing things.

We've all been fooling around with media for our entire lives, and we've learned a tremendous amount about the world and about media in the process. Of course, there's a lot more to a media education program than just fooling around, but when you come to teaching students how to use the video camera, say, and you are tempted to give them a list of the names of all the parts of the machine, followed by a test on those names, think back to the time you were learning to ride a bicycle. How useful was a list of bicycle part names to you then? What you needed then was information about safety and practice in an environment free from criticism and other dangers.

Fooling around definitely has an important place in the curriculum. However, it's doubtful anyone ever learned the uses of the semi-colon by being encouraged to doodle semi-colons for hours on end. There are certainly times and situations when fooling around will not do.

Eventually, you will want your students to have some awareness of their own levels of ability in handling skills and tools for making and examining media texts. The skills they need are not identical to those of media professionals, and the tools and equipment they need will not be the same as those available to professionals. But that's OK. You can become a good driver whether you learn in a Chevrolet or in a Cadillac.

We already have many skills to help us understand how media texts are put together, and how they work. Our homes, schools and businesses are well equipped with tools that help us to receive, manipulate and make media messages. Capitalizing on this existing inventory will refine and expand media education. Naturally, we'd all prefer to have generous budgets to help us equip our media classrooms with VCR's, monitors, projectors, cameras, editing suites, computers and all the paraphernalia we'd love to have. But the reality is that budgets are too tight to allow for this level of equipping schools, and media education is too important to be left off the curriculum until the budgets are available. Some of the equipment that we are convinced we need is equipment that we ourselves do not know how to use. Remember, you don't need it until you need it, and when you absolutely need it, you'll either get it or find another way of doing the job. Or the students will. We have to be inventive scavengers in our media teaching. My own preference would be to mange without some resources than to get them through some sponsorship or partnership program that required me and the school to offer up students as captive audiences for in-school advertising. (See **TEACHING MEDIA ON THE CHEAP**)

SCREENING

IMAGES

Media educators and students should be aware not only of the process of media perception itself but also of what I call the screens that exist in that process. I'm using the word screen here as a gardener or an electrical engineer would use it: as some sort of a mesh through which things have to pass during a process; and as some sort of an instrument that modifies what it allows to pass through it, by sorting out or filtering different parts of the medium. What comes through one side of the screen is a bit different from what went in at the other side.

Media educators can apply this analogy to perception. I have already mentioned that media messages are constructions: they are carefully put together by groups of people who know how to represent things to their best advantage in particular media. Political reporters, for instance, know how to slant their work so that the story strokes their readers' preferences and prejudices. People who make rock videos or commercials work very hard to package their messages for specific audiences. Any media image - for example, say from a news broadcast - is altered by the fact that the news program is sponsored by an industry of media broadcasting, which stays in business by relying on its own sponsors, either commercial or governmental. The industry is governed also by ideologies and technical standards. Each of the components that goes into the constructing of a media message can be seen as a kind of a screen that the message has passed through, and which, in turn, has modified the message in some way or another. Since these screens are part of the media construction, then part of the media consumer's job is to be aware of them and of their influence. This is the process of deconstruction.

Other screens exist in the perceiver, in the part of the process that we have called reconstruction and also in the construction part of the process where the meaning is rebuilt. To a large extent, the sum total of a person's non-visual information becomes one of the most important screens within the media consumer. The siren example given in the last section is an instance of the influence of a screen within the perceiver influencing the construction of meaning. Ideology is another screen that exists within the perceiver (as well as in the media message), and is one that can lead to very divergent interpretations of media texts. (This video is sexist. That movie is excellent. I refuse to read that newspaper.)

These screens are the component parts of media education - the conceptual frameworks or key concepts that are readily available to media educators through such resources as:

> the Ontario Ministry of Education's *Media Literacy resource Document*, (1989), which lists eight key concepts;

> Len Masterman, a British scholar, whose book *Teaching the Media*, (COMEDIA, 1989) has been one of the most important influences on contemporary media education, suggests (page 23-24) a list of 27 key concepts;

> the British Film Institute, whose two documents, *Primary Media Education, a Curriculum Statement*, (edited by Cary Bazalgette, 1989) and *Secondary Media Education, a Curriculum Statement*, (edited by Julian Bowker, 1991) list six key concepts for elementary for secondary school media teachers.

> Many provinces and states now offer lists of "benchmarks", "outcomes" or "standards" which can be found either quoted or linked in The Media Awareness Network at: http://www.media-awareness.ca/eng/sitemap.html

All these different versions have enough in common for the media educator to feel quite comfortable in adapting or adopting any one or all of them. But I feel that the media education classroom is a more viable and exciting place when key concepts are constantly explored and challenged. Once the teacher has decided that one list of key concepts is superior to another, and begins to work year after year from that one list, some of the edge has gone from the practice of media education. I suppose my preference would be to develop or fine tune a new list of concepts in co-operation with each class, a recommendation that you will find supported in Masterman's work.

In the light of this, the organization of key concepts or screens that I am about to describe must be taken as draft. Some readers will recognize changes in it from the last time they heard me speak about it. If you were to talk to me tomorrow, you might find I have made more changes. (There are changes in this second edition of *Screening Images.*) We have to accept such changes as part of our continuous learning.

SCREEN #1:   MEDIA ARE INDUSTRIES

Every media message that we receive is the product of an industry. Someone controls that industry and may, in turn, be influenced by others who exercise another kind of control. The owners of the industry have objectives and purposes they are trying to fulfil. Successful media industries know exactly what they are doing, and perceptive media consumers need to be aware of the industry's agenda. It may frequently be harmless and benign, or it may occasionally be dangerous and manipulative. Unless you take the trouble to figure it out, you may not be aware which is which. There are basically seven companies who own almost all the mass media production and distribution facilities in north America:

> Music:
>> Sony
>> Seagrams
> Movies, TV and Radio:
>> Viacom – Paramount
>> General Electric – NBC
>> Westinghouse – CBS
>> Disney – ABC
>> Time/Warner/Turner

This concentration of ownership in the media industries has profound effects on the way the media operate and on the way they address their audiences.

All media are expensive to produce and to distribute. Somehow the outlay of money has to be recouped.

Questions to ask are:
>> who's in charge here?
>> what do they want of me, and why?

what else do they want?
how much did this cost, and who pays the bills?

SCREEN #2:   MEDIA TEXTS ARE CONSTRUCTED
PRODUCTS

We have already talked about how texts are constructions. In media, the construction goes beyond the unconscious assigning of codes to meaning, into the realm of deliberate choices for distinct purposes. Things like genre, convention and technique come into play in this category. Part of the process of deconstruction is the recognition, conscious or unconscious, of these components.

Questions to ask are:

what kind of text is this?
what conventions does it follow/break?
how is it put together?

SCREEN #3:   THE AUDIENCE IS PART OF THE MEDIA TEXT

In constructing media texts, media makers take their audience into account very seriously. Assumptions are made about who is attending to the text, and about what that audience expects from the text. The text varies depending on these assumptions.

Questions to ask are:
who is this intended for?
what expectations do text and audience have of each other?
who am I assumed to be?

SCREEN #4:   MEDIA TEXTS CONTAIN VALUES

Media texts cannot help but reflect the values of the people who make them. Sometimes the values are up front and obvious, as in a televised debate. Sometimes the values or ideology are hidden in the sub-text, and take some digging out.

Questions to ask are:
how real is this text?
how and where do I find the meaning?

what values are being presented?
what commercial messages are included here?
what political messages?
what social messages?
what artistic messages?

SCREEN #5:   AUDIENCES REACT TO DIFFERENT TEXTS IN DIFFERENT WAYS DEPENDING ON THEIR PREDISPOSITION

No individuals or groups are entirely alike. Each audience will react to each text in a different way. Sometimes the same audience will react to the same text in different ways on different occasions.

Questions to ask are:

what`s my predisposition towards this text?
do I assent by agreeing or liking?
do I resist by disagreeing or disliking?
do I negotiate by working with the text to understand my reaction better?

SCREEN #6:   AUDIENCES RESPOND TO TEXTS BY FITTING THEM INTO THEIR OWN SYSTEMS OF PERCEPTION

Audiences use this screen to make matches between their own non-visual information and the text. This is the key screen for personal response.

Questions to ask are:

how does the text fit with my own experience/values/ beliefs/ ideology/needs/hopes/fears?

SCREEN #7:   AUDIENCES USE SKILLS IN INTERPRETING MEDIA TEXTS

This screen helps to account for some of the differences between responses of different audience members. Some people are more skilled than others at deconstructing and reconstructing texts, and this makes a difference. Some audiences are skilled at reflecting on their response to a text, and others are not.

Questions to ask are:

> what skills of de/reconstruction do I need to apply to this text?
> what new skills do I need to learn in order to react to this text?

The screens mentioned above are included in the diagram on the next page.

Each of these screens changes the text or the audience's perception of the text to some degree so that what the audience finally makes of it has been modified by perhaps six different screens, some that exist in the text, and others in the audience. The more knowledgeable, perceptive and reflective audiences become about the influences of these screens upon their response to media texts, the more media literate those audiences can be called. Media education is largely about helping audiences come to terms with these screens and their influence as those same audiences consume, examine or make media texts.

Be careful of thinking of skills as the whole story. Skills in media education, as in any other subject, are only enablers to learning, they are not the learning itself.

SCREENING IMAGES FRAMEWORK

MEDIA TEXT	
INDUSTRY------------	Who's in charge What do they want of me? Why? What else do they want? How much does it cost? Who pays?
PRODUCT-------------	What kind of text is this/ Conventions followed/broken? How is this constructed?
AUDIENCE------------	Who's this intended for? What expectations between text and audience? Who am I supposed to be?
VALUES-----------------	How real is this text? How/where do I find meaning? What values are presented? What is the $$ message? What's the ideology here? Social/political/artistic?
PREDISPOSITION----	Assent? Resist? Negotiate? How do I fit this into my personal world?
SKILLS-----------------	What skills do I apply to this? De/reconstruction? New skills required?

RECEIVER----------------------------What's it all mean in the end?

IT'S WHAT WE MAKE OF IT THAT COUNTS.
ALL LEARNING IS AN ACT OF CONSTRUCTION

SCREENING IMAGES

If we overlay the concept of the screens on the process of media text perception (construction, deconstruction, reconstruction, construction) we can create a composite that represents a scheme of media perception as shown in the diagram below..

This model of how media study works still lacks one important detail. That detail has more to do with learning than with media, but it is one of the most important components of any classroom in any subject, and deserves a short section to itself. It is called "metacognition".

PROCESS OF TEXT PERCEPTION

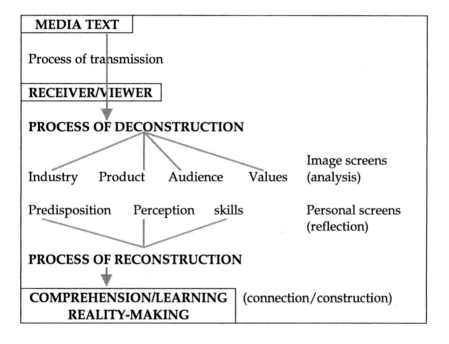

KNOWING HOW

YOU KNOW

Metacognition is a fancy name for knowing what you know and how you come to know it. Knowledge itself is wonderful, but it is enhanced when we can make ourselves more aware of our knowing. Let's take an example. Say you had just solved a fairly complex problem and were feeling pretty proud of yourself, until you realized that you weren't really aware of how you'd done it, and couldn't, therefore, solve the next problem. You've just realized that the conscious knowledge of how to solve all problems of this type is more valuable to you than this one answer.

When my middle son was about five, I once asked him to do some mental task that was way beyond his years, proud but foolish father that I was. His answer floored me: "Daddy," he said, "I don't know how to know that yet!" He was infuriatingly right, of course, and his response revealed more than his knowledge of my error: it showed his awareness of his own scope of abilities and potential. This is metacognition.

More and more in modern curriculum, teachers are asked to help students become aware of their own processes of learning. The process conference approach is one way we use to teach writing, and we encourage small group learning in all areas of the curriculum as a way for students to approach new information. Teachers in many areas have discovered the value of the learning log as a way of helping students consolidate their understanding of their day's work. Self and peer evaluation are encouraged widely to engage students in examining and assessing their own learning and achievement. For such process-oriented systems to work, there has to be a part of the program that makes the students aware, through reflection, of what the actual processes are and of how they as students fit into them, and take advantage of them.

There are educational theorists who claim that education

should consist of nothing that is not factual. With Joe Friday-like insistence, they demand that anything to do with process, conjecture or reflection has no place in schools. "Just give them the facts", is their war cry. Let me say at once that I categorically disagree with this view of education. I believe that the ability to analyze process, and to use it to one's own learning advantage, the flexibility that is bred by practice with conjecture and "what if..?" scenarios, and the mental and human growth that are promoted through reflection, are among the most useful and vital things that students learn in schools today. Many business people I know agree. They tell me that they would much rather have an employee skilled as a learner than one who has just got hold of a big bunch of knowledge and skills.

Don't get me wrong: I'm not against content. It would be silly to promote the writing process if students did not write, and foolish to have them write without having them write about something. It's generally true that learners are more interested in product than in process. A media student is naturally anxious about the audio tape she is producing, while the teacher is possibly more concerned about what she is learning in making it. The teacher also wants the student to be conscious about her learning so that she will be able to use it more readily the next time.

Knowing how you know something and being able to articulate that knowledge helps you get ready to know the next thing. For instance, if two students were asked how they knew that the word "bomb" ended in a "b", and one answered: "I don't know. I just knew," and the other said: "Well, I always think of it as being connected to other words like "bombard", or "bombardier" and then the "b" makes sense," which one is the better speller? Which one is the better learner?

From one point of view, both could spell the word, and therefore they are equally good at spelling that word. From another point of view, though, the second student who was able to reflect on the personal process of knowing that particular spelling is showing an awareness that is likely to have more than this one application. This awareness could very well serve that student in another hundred learning situations in which the other student would not be able to fall back on an explanation like, "I just knew." Come to think of it, "I just knew" sounds an awful lot as if the student might have been relying on memory power, rather than on brain power. My personal view of education requires me to concentrate on developing both, but more on the latter than on the former.

Ideas for Media Education

Reflection ought to be a major part of all curriculum, and all classes and activities should provide students with the time to think back over processes and class work to find answers to questions such as:

- how did we do that?
- how did I know that?
- what was important about this piece of learning?
- how can I use this again, now that I know how to do it?
- what is this connected to?
- is this a new skill I've learned?
- what comes next?

Much of this can be achieved through the simple provision of time at the end of a group task, for instance, for the group to reflect on how well it functioned, what it achieved and how, how it could have done better, or just differently. Conferences between teachers and students over project work should contain a component of this same kind of reflection, as should peer conferences. Allowing students to be responsible for part of the assessment of their own and each others' work is another way of encouraging metacognition, since the act of justifying an opinion or a judgment forces a person to bring the skills, knowledge and processes of knowing to the front of their consciousness. (See Worsnop, Chris M, *ASSESSING MEDIA WORK: Authentic Assessment in Media Education*, Wright Communications, 1996)

One of the most important questions that you should ask in your classroom, and which you should insist that students regularly ask of themselves and of each other is:

"HOW DO I KNOW?"

Let's go back to our SCREENING IMAGES FRAMEWORK, then, and put the finishing touches to it, by adding that important question at every opportunity that presents itself.

Much of the meaning and understanding that students get from media education will be about media; some of the rest will be

SCREENING IMAGES

about the world in general; and not a small part will be about themselves. All three kinds of understanding play off and contribute to one another, and no program is complete unless it encourages all three.

SCREENING IMAGES FRAMEWORK

MEDIA TEXT	
INDUSTRY-----------	Who's in charge
	What do they want of me? Why?
	What else do they want?
	How much does it cost? Who pays?
	HOW DO I KNOW?
PRODUCT-----------	What kind of text is this/
	Conventions followed/broken?
	How is this constructed?
	HOW DO I KNOW?
AUDIENCE---------	Who's this intended for?
	?
	Who am I supposed to be?
	HOW DO I KNOW?
VALUES-----------	How real is this text?
	How/where do I find meaning?
	What values are presented?
	What is the $$ message?
	What's the ideology here?
	Social/political/artistic?
	HOW DO I KNOW?
PREDISPOSITION-	Assent?
	Resist?
	Negotiate?
	HOW DO I KNOW?
SKILLS----------	What skills do I apply to this?
	De/reconstruction?
	New skills required?
	HOW DO I KNOW?

RECEIVER-----------------**What's it all mean in the end?**
HOW DO I KNOW?

IT'S WHAT WE MAKE OF IT THAT COUNTS.
ALL LEARNING IS AN ACT OF CONSTRUCTION

ORTHODOXY
IS
THE ENEMY

An orthodoxy is a strong point of view. It often starts from a philosophy or an ideology, and ends up as a way of seeing the entire world. Some orthodoxies come from religions, some from politics, others from charismatic individuals in all walks of life. People who hold to an orthodoxy are prone to extreme, dogmatic and inflexible thinking. There are orthodoxies in teaching, such as phonics-first and look-say approaches to beginning reading, and there are orthodoxies in media education that can lead the unwary media teacher into all kinds of swampy territory.

ORTHODOXY #1: MEDIA EDUCATION AS CIVIL DEFENSE

There's a way of thinking about media, and of presenting them in the classroom, that is based on the orthodoxy that the media are bad for you and that you need to be protected from them by a cuirass of knowledge about the detailed nature of their evil. You may have noticed an irony in the fact that some of the people who decry the wickedness of the media do so on TV, frequently on Sunday mornings. Neil Postman, the *Education as a Subversive/Conserving Activity* man, has written a book called *Amusing Ourselves to Death,*(Viking, 1985) in which he sounds a Chicken-Little call that our society has succeeded in spawning yet another dastardly influence that will undermine its very moral fibre and lead to its downfall. A partial list of all these spawnings during my own lifetime would have to include such degenerate phenomena as: horror comics, ball point pens, Elvis Presley, hooped skirts, Go-Go girls, *The Catcher in the Rye,* narrow trouser bottoms, Chubby Checker, Coca Cola, *Playboy,* electronic calculators, bell bottomed trousers, mini skirts, rock 'n roll, video arcades, computers, Club Med, the Beatles, maxi skirts, headbands,

28

draft dodgers, *The Diviners*, Walkmans, ghetto blasters, Much Music, *Miami Vice*, Nintendo, cellular phones.... You get the picture.

You have probably seen it a hundred times if you have seen it once: the great TV statistic. You know, the one that tells us that today's children have watched more TV than they have eaten breakfasts; spent more time in front of the TV than in school; seen more films than they've had conversations; and so on.

One of the most recent manifestation of this orthodoxy is called "the prevention approach". It is based on concerns and assumptions of public health such as: media content is a cause of social ills like violence, teen pregnancy, bad language, drug abuse etc. Media education is seen as a cure for these ills, or at least as a tool in the cure. People stake out extreme positions at the polar ends of this view of media-as-cause and lob missiles at each other from their entrenched positions, asserting their certain knowledge that media do or do not cause social behavior. (See **TV AS SICKNESS** in Part Two)

Children today are certainly more influenced by TV than my parents were, but they are perhaps less influenced by it than their own parents (and perhaps even their grandparents) were at the same age. This is not the first or even the second TV generation to hit the schools. Still, many of those statistics about hours watched and such are based on the number of hours the TV set is turned on in a house, with a gigantic leap of faith involved in concluding that everyone, or even someone is watching the darned thing.

You will probably be able to name more than one person who actually does seem to be negatively influenced by extreme exposure to TV, and you may well believe that rationing TV or even banning some of its manifestations would be a boon to our society and to many individuals in it. But if you do, then I urge you to beware of the orthodoxy in which a perfectly good idea or philosophy is turned into a compulsory and inflexible system to be followed at all costs.

If you get on board with this orthodoxy, you will find yourself at odds with much of today's popular culture, and with the young people who find their diversion and entertainment in it. In short, you'll have isolated yourself from the very people you are trying to influence. Media education will have been turned into another of those school subjects in which the students' knowledge and ideas are valued less than the teacher's. Success will be assessed not so much in terms of originality and daring as in terms of measuring up to the orthodoxy.

SCREENING IMAGES

Where, you might ask, are the counterbalancing claims about all the benefits we get from being a media society? Do we really believe that the Vietnam war, Watergate, Irangate etc. would have been subject to such public scrutiny without the media? (If the media were not so influential in these instances, how do we explain the concerted effort of the authorities to avoid the Vietnam influences during the Granada and Panama invasions, the Falklands war or the Gulf or Kosovo wars, with such fascinating results for the student of media?)

Would we willingly deprive ourselves of all the excellence in the media, including TV, just to be rid of the unabashed junk? (If we could agree, that is, about what is junk and what is not.) And do we fool ourselves into believing that if we were successful in getting rid of one batch of junk there would not immediately arise a new batch to take its place? Who is hypocrite enough to pretend that they themselves do not enjoy junk from time to time?

If we approach media education in the classroom with this civil defence attitude, then there is an almost sure-fire guarantee that students will switch us off, counting our dire warnings as just another manifestation of adult paranoia and lack of understanding. No, we cannot teach media in the classroom from an orthodox aim of "improving our students' taste in media". That is just the old aim of teaching middle class values dressed up in new garb. The minute we criticize the stuff kids like to read, watch or listen to as being in some way inferior, we have lost their attention, pushed them into an attitude of rejecting our values as strongly as we reject theirs, turned media education into another dreary trip through *Lorna Doone* or *Moby Dick*.

ORTHODOXY #2: MEDIA EDUCATION AS IDEOLOGICAL MEANS TEST

In some ways the corollary to the civil defense approach to media education is the approach that subjects every piece of media content to some sort of suitability test based upon the ideology that underpins it. It doesn't matter what set of ideals you are trying to promote with this particular form of selection; the point is that you are going to present an incomplete view of the world, and exclude many excellent pieces of media work, simply because they do not agree with an orthodox ideology. You are going to be propagandizing your students.

The leftists, for instance, will want to bathe the students in media that dump on acid rain, free trade, pro-life, globalization and similar issues. This group might perhaps censor out of their students' experience the films of Leni Reifenstahl, or the writings of Wm. F. Buckley JR., simply because these people's works stand outside the official orthodoxy.

Rightists would look for media to support a different set of values, and would want nothing to do with the films of Arthur Penn, the books of John Steinbeck, liberal-minded TV programs such as *Star Trek*, anything on the CBC, or from the editorial pages of the *Toronto Star*.

This kind of selection is nothing less than a form of censorship, and results not in media education so much as media conditioning.

If this orthodoxy were restricted to political or philosophical ideas, it would be relatively easy to deal with, but today, ideologies that begin with political, philosophical or religious ideas extend into areas related to race, gender, sexual orientation and class, into issues like equity and voice, and into topics like abortion, welfare and economics.

The danger in media education when it comes to ideology is to present a course in which only one ideology, or even one narrow band of one ideology is acceptable or "correct". To succeed in the course students don't have to learn to think for themselves so much as to think like the teacher. Imposing this kind of orthodoxy on students is crippling.

Of course it would be silly in media education to pretend that ideologies did not exist or that they did not influence the media. It would, perhaps, be criminal. Ignoring ideology is no better than pushing a single ideology. The only tenable stance towards ideology is one which helps students identify ideological influences in their media, clarify their own ideological beliefs, and come to terms with the way that ideologies operate within the media. The course should focus on the strengths and weaknesses of various ideological stances as they appear in the media, showing respect for difference. In the end we have to acknowledge that the course is one in media, not in ideology.

ORTHODOXY #3: MEDIA EDUCATION AS MULTIPLICATION TABLES

Perhaps you've come across a few of the publications that treat media education as if it were a set of new multiplication tables to be memorized. I'm thinking of the approach to media that assumes everything has to be reduced to lists of terms and techniques to be memorized and tested; that bases its approach on the unstated assumption that artists consciously work from lists of techniques and terminologies in creating their work, and that students must know the grammar of each medium in order to be qualified to study it.

This approach assumes that students cannot study photographs or pictures until after they have learnt all about composition and cameras. The study of film becomes the memorizing of the names given to camera shots and angles. Newspaper study degenerates into learning off the jargon of journalism. The study of TV is reduced to a list of facts about studio set ups. The nation needs more kids who know the difference between a cut and a fade. (Or substitute: who can list off seven characteristics of the ballad; who can define and give one example of zeugma; who can recite the difference between a gerund and a gerundive.)

The orthodoxy here is one that denies the value of investigative learning, that puts the teacher solely in charge of the classroom's entire agenda, and that believes that the students learn only what is directly taught to them. This orthodoxy has its corollary in the approach which forbids teachers ever to intervene in students' learning, for fear of interfering with natural processes. As orthodoxies, both are literally stifling to students who are trying to do an efficient job of learning; but both can also be liberating when used judiciously.

If a student asks a question like, "How does the emulsion get onto the film?" a teacher might well teach a compact, informative mini-lesson on the topic. Another teacher might guide the student to resources where the information can easily be found. Another might merely say "Find out for yourself, and prepare a short report for the class." Any of these responses might be perfectly valid, providing they came from an orientation that considers the student and the context of the question, rather than from an inflexible belief about where knowledge comes from or how students learn.

It isn't enough for students to have just some easy, technical kind of knowledge about their culture, nor is it important for them to acquire this kind of knowledge before they go on to do anything else. Unless there has been a time in class when the effect of a fade on a TV screen became an important issue, or when a student had a good reason to want to use one in a class project, then there is no reason to bring up the term at all. Arguing that kids can't understand the media without knowing the terminology first is like saying that it's necessary to understand how the Muppets are worked by their handlers before you can watch *Sesame Street* properly.

On the other hand, if we put watching *Sesame Street* first, and progress from there to *inquiring* about the puppets, then we have a learning situation. Learning situations can be very different from instructing situations.

ORTHODOXY #4: MEDIA CRITICISM 301

Look out for the great literary criticism trap, in which the media are seen merely as alternatives to books - and who knows books better than us English teachers? - and therefore are to be treated in the same way as books: hunt the Christ figure; seek the symbol; uproot the archetype; find the myth; identify the auteur; explore the genre. In this approach the teacher is empowered by being possessed of a kind of knowledge that the kids don't have because they haven't taken the second and third year university courses in which the teacher learned it. This helps teachers to feel important. It also helps teachers to keep control by preventing the study at hand from taking off in unanticipated directions. It's dull and weary, won't do the media any good at all, and certainly will do very little to help students to a better understanding of the media world in which they swim.

How many people do you really know who tune into their favorite TV show because of its "Jungian echoes", or who select the movies they'll see on the grounds of how faithful they are to archetypal patterns? Such considerations are valid, but their validity is academic. They are even important, but their importance is chiefly for adults and scholars of criticism. Let's leave them in the advanced university courses where they belong, and let's hide our own overt knowledge of critical terminology from children rather than flaunt it or require them to parrot it. When we want to communicate with students on equal terms, it's far better for us to construct a terminology together to suit our joint needs.

CONCLUSION

Media education ought to be an exploration. The teachers should be exploring as much as the students, and should be learning the same amount, perhaps more. The concept of co-learning that is common in the literature of gifted education is a very useful concept for teachers of media education. A teacher who knows nothing or little about a topic does not need to feel inadequate in front of a class of students. The skill of the teacher resides in the ability to help young people learn. That is our profession.

Teachers and students should approach the media as inquiry. Their objectives should be to see what questions turn out to be important about the media, what methods they can devise to find out the answers, and then what the answers turn out to be. There would be no contradiction if the teacher habitually steered the class in the direction of a useful piece of information, a concept, or in a way that required the exercise of a new skill.

There would almost certainly be times when the teacher would find it profitable and wise to arrange for a class on terminology, or ideology, or civil defense, or critical theory; but those occasions should arise from the questions raised in the class rather than from the fact that it is the third Tuesday in November. Those classes might just as easily be taught by some of the students as by the teacher, for, frequently, the students will be in the know when the teachers are in the dark.

We should be careful of the trap of assuming that there are going to be right and wrong answers to the questions that are raised. Right and wrong is far too narrow a spectrum of possibility for responses if we are to encourage real inquiry. But we can be sure that there will be good learning and weak learning; worthwhile investigation and poor investigation; clear thinking and muddled thinking. Helping students differentiate among these produces outcomes worth placing at the head of the educational agenda in any classroom.

If this itself is an orthodoxy, then it's one I can live with more easily than the others.

PART TWO

IDEAS ABOUT

MEDIA

(AND EDUCATION)

SCREENING IMAGES

CHILDREN, PARENTS, TEACHERS AND MEDIA EDUCATION

Scarcely anybody questions the good sense in helping their young children learn to read. The daily press is filled with articles critical of the levels of print literacy among our youngsters, and tends to put the blame squarely on the shoulders of what it calls a "failed public education system". Many families, having prepared their children well for a world filled with print and for the enjoyment of it are puzzled by these attacks, and turn their attention not so much to the education system as to the media.

Society is filled with messages from the mass media; we have radio, TV, film, video, fashion, advertising, newspapers, magazines, junk mail, video games and all the good stuff now emerging from the Internet. While it has been enough in the past for families to help their children come to terms with the intricacies of the alphabet - reading, spelling and the enjoyment of books - we need to ask if that is still enough.

It is common these days for the joy of the shared bedtime story to be replaced with the isolation of the solitary bedtime TV or video. The language games and songs that used to fill the tedious hours on long car journeys have often given way to the beeps and squeaks of hand-held video- games or personal radio-tape headsets. These things are not bad in themselves, but if we allow them to take over our children's lives and imaginations without comment or action from us, they can become negative influences.

I do not intend to hold up our media-filled world as one of evil and high danger. I do not blame the changes in our modern society on the media. I do, though, claim that we can live more comfortably and with more happiness in our modern world if we understand the things that are going on, and if we come to terms with change and with the media which bring us the messages about our society, about change and about ourselves; in short, I promote the practice of media education - the understanding of how the media work, how we interact with them and how we can make the most of them. I suggest that much of the understanding of our mediated world can be achieved happily and with enjoyment, without stern moralizing or didacticism.

Answer these few questions for yourself to see if you should read on:

- Do you want your children to grow up thinking for themselves, making wise decisions, solving problems independently, operating from a positive value system they have constructed themselves through experience and interaction with others?
- Do you believe that our mass media world contains many benefits of life, a great deal of happiness and pleasure, considerable beauty and plenty wisdom, as well as large helpings of escapist junk?
- Is your mind still open on questions which probe the relationships between media violence and violence in society; sexual content in the media and sexual behavior; representations of anti-social behavior and social deviance?
- And finally, are you comfortable with diversity of opinions within your own family? Do you accept - but not encourage - that family members who think things through on their own might arrive at conclusions, opinions and beliefs which may differ from your own?

If any of the questions above rub you the wrong way, make you react with a "Hurrummph!" instead of a "Ahaaah!" or just plain made you angry, then you might be wise to move to a new chapter now. You may not like the way this one raises questions without offering for-certain answers; explores possibilities without making value judgments; suggests that figuring things out is as valuable as being told a fixed answer by someone else.

There are occasions in everyday life that offer chances for us to learn about media, about society and about life. The chapters in this section are reflections and narratives: they tell stories of my own family experience as a child and as an adult. These stories often begin with a trivial experience such as a trip through a family photo album with one of my children, and then proceed through reflection to examine a lesson in media education that might conclude with an insight like, "the camera always lies". Sometimes the reflections are prompted by a cataclysm, a war, an earthquake, a famine, a riot or - to be more accurate - by the versions of these events that are presented to us by the media.

Ideas for Media Education

A person who has got media education is someone who understands the media. It's someone who knows how the media work to bring news, facts, information, products and entertainment to us. You can get this information and understanding without memorizing a lot of specialized terms about media, and without studying media in any systematic or sequential fashion.

Media education isn't something that makes people cynical about media. It may make them skeptical, but I think it's a good idea for consumers of popular culture to be honestly skeptical about everything that is offered to them as representing knowledge, fact, information or entertainment. After all, consuming popular culture is really very little different from consuming any other product. You need to know which is the good stuff and which is not so good, or you could end up consuming a bunch of garbage. The effects of a diet of garbage media can be every bit as debilitating as the consumption of any other kinds of garbage. People should develop the habit of always questioning their sources of information.

I am a strong believer that children can develop much of this media education awareness in the same way they develop their readiness for reading. They do it in conversation with their family; they do it through shared experience, discussion, exploration and reflection with family members and with friends. Very often the lessons are accidental, but sometimes a person will go to unusual lengths to bring a media lesson to someone else. This can happen when we recommend a TV program to a friend, share a newspaper or magazine article, help someone select a new article of clothing while shopping, or talk over a news story over coffee.

An undergraduate teacher of mine said in class, more years ago than I will admit, "we must all learn to control language, or most assuredly it will end up controlling us." Western societies believe very strongly in language education and devote massive resources in their school systems to teaching children how to read and write, and to a lesser extent, to listen and speak. Not very long ago, the ability to read write, listen and speak gave an individual the power to participate in all the major communications available in society. But with the invention of photography and the cinema in the late 19th century, and then the radio, recorded music, TV, and the personal computer in the 20th, citizens have been taking part in societies that are ever more complex and ever less reliant on the spoken and written word.

SCREENING IMAGES

Yet our education systems still insist that language literacy is the chief - and sometimes the only - literacy that students need. They pay scarce attention to any other kinds of literacy: children are not taught how to "read" and "write" using television images or audio recordings. Computer courses often emphasize employability skills at the expense of understanding. Media education is needed so that society can have citizens who can control the dominant media in their lives, to avoid being controlled by them.

Most parents instinctively know how to teach some of the most important lessons in media education. When we teach our children to read using picture books, we show them pictures that contain meaning. Children can follow a picture long before they can unlock meaning from print. When we watch TV in our children's company, and indulge in family chatter about what a dumb piece of dialogue that was, or how funny that situation became, or how stereotyped that character is, or talk to each other about what we bet will happen next and how we know, we're teaching our children how to watch TV.

When we sit on the weekend with our newspapers, carefully going through some sections and discarding others without opening them - I open the sports section only during the baseball season - children learn what it is to be selective. When we make a point of buying a certain magazine, or of watching a specific news program, children learn that media have uses other than entertainment.

When we take our children to the movies, and later talk about the story, the special effects, the music, the costumes, the make-up or the acting, children learn that media messages are constructed very carefully by their authors. When we disagree about what is pleasurable in media and what is not, children learn that systems of values are needed to discriminate among all the possible media pieces available to them.

I offer the following stories to you as evidence of what we have learned and experienced. I do not expect that they are bound to have an identical effect on you, but I do hope that you find them interesting, entertaining at times, stimulating and occasionally instructive. You may even find one or two of them that seem to contradict each other – which is OK by me. It's an enigmatic world. (For instance, compare this chapter with **YOUTH CRITICISM 101**.) I would hate to think that you got to the end of this book and decided your time had been completely wasted.

ADVICE
AND
CAVEATS

Let's ask some very basic questions. Why are we teaching media at all? What are our objectives? Are we looking to produce students who know a lot of facts about the different media? Are we interested in preparing students for eventual careers in the media? Do we want students to appreciate the academic aspects that we can find in the media, such as media history or theories of media criticism? I suppose we could answer a modified "yes" to all of those questions, or a modified "no". We could say "yes" because it would be good for students to develop some knowledge and skills along any of these lines, and difficult to teach media without coming close to each of them. We could say "no" because no one of these objectives is important enough to justify a media education program. My answer to the question, (you knew I'd eventually get round to it) is this: we teach media because the media are an important part of our environment, and it is irresponsible not to study one's environment.

An environment consists of many components: it has an economy, a social structure, a political structure, a culture, a legal system, and several different kinds of ecology. The media play an important part in all of these environmental components, and in order to understand the environment, we have to understand the media's role in it.

Outstanding examples of mass media as part of our environment are constantly passing before our eyes as satellite reports reach us from events in places like Tienanmen Square, the Gulf war, Sarajevo (but not from East Timor). The answer to the questions, "Who decides whether the satellite feed to the western news media will be cut off, and how are those decisions made?" would provide material for many a fruitful investigation of how we receive the material that we call news, and how the flow of it is controlled on our behalf. Of course, these situations raise a number of other very interesting media

41

questions, such as: where did the students in Tienanmen Square get their vision of democracy? Why are some of the signs in demonstrations all over the world written in English? In whose interest is it to control the flow of information about events such as these? In whose interest is it to open up the flow of information?

Other questions could well be such as: What actually happened in these locations? How do we know? What might have happened that we do not know? What sort of information do we as consumers of news have at our disposal in order to make decisions about our own view of these events? Which images of these events remain with us, and how were they constructed for maximum impact? (Remember the young man in Tienanmen Square confronting the tank armed only with pamphlets . . .?)

Here then are some points to help you organize your media education courses:

THINGS TO DO:

- Always be prepared to work with all the media.
- Be clear about your objectives for teaching the media, and focus your sessions on them and the key concepts rather than on one specific medium, or even on a theme. (Although a theme can be an important vehicle for these objectives)
- The more you can integrate media education into other subject areas, the more you are likely to be able to convince students that this is more than just another dumb subject full of stuff to be remembered.
- Remember how important it is not to approach the media as if you are saving the students from decadence by giving them the benefit of your superior taste.
- Seize the moment. When another Tiananmen or Kosovo happens, change your plans and address your teaching objectives by using the breaking news story.
- Show films/videos (mostly) without interruption.
- Save student assignments for a time after they have seen the complete work.
- Provide time for thought and talk before asking for feedback after a video/film presentation.
- Try to have the students voice their own viewpoints, always being reluctant to give your own first.
- Make sure to give respect to all students' points of view.

- Use small group work, drama, problem-solving and decision-making exercises frequently.
- Expand the objectives of your program beyond knowledge and skills.
- Treat all media as equal in value. Be especially careful not to treat print as being superior, or TV as the only mass medium.
- Teach historically when it's suitable, but don't base your course on chronology. In media, the present is most important.
- Some of your favorite films/videos from the decades of your own youth and early career are no doubt excellent and important, but remember the age of your students.

THINGS TO AVOID

- Avoid the mistakes of the literati who taught the theories of literary criticism thinking they were teaching literature.
- Avoid the mistakes of the Socrates groupies who believed that the only way to teach was with question and answer sessions.
- Avoid the mistakes of the grammarians who mistook a set of prescriptive rules and terminologies for the true content of the language curriculum.
- Avoid the mistakes of the psychometricians who assumed that the whole was merely the sum of its parts, and that the parts could and should be mastered by all, at the same speed, in the same order.
- Avoid the mistakes of the lecturers who went on and on about their own interpretation or that of their guru, shutting out all else.
- Avoid the mistake of the anthology makers, who assumed that they should make all the choices.
- Avoid the Friday afternoon mistake - all through the week.
- Avoid the mistake of the Bloom generation, who assumed that a taxonomy was a sequence, and who

programmed everything into easily masticated mastery modules.

- Avoid the mistake of the mathematicians who thought learning was a search for nothing but right answers.
- Avoid the mistake of the academics who assumed that there was only one kind of learning to value, the cognitive kind.

TAKING
A
SECOND LOOK

How long do you spend looking at your morning paper? Do you, or other people you know, tend to turn to another TV program as soon as you realize that you've already seen the one you're watching? Are you one of the millions of people in the industrialized world who possesses a collection of video tapes of movies and programs that you fully intend to watch some day as soon as you get around to it? Ditto books and magazines? Do you have a tendency to try to pursue more than one activity at a time: turning the pages of a magazine as you watch TV; listening to music as you do your homework; playing the radio as you drive; talking on the cellular phone as you eat (heaven forbid!) in a restaurant; do you combine watching a movie in a theatre with conversation, flirting, target practice or confectionery shopping?

If you can answer "yes" to some of these questions, then you are not only normal, but you are a typical consumer of media messages. You tend to give things a single chance to communicate with you, or sometimes with the part of you that is attending. You are capable of bilocation and multiple tasking. You are a modern person.

Media makers know that you are like that, and so they often adapt their message accordingly. Newspapers are now designed so that the reader's eye can quickly scan the pages in search of an article or advertisement that attracts their attention. Many TV programs summarize their action-so-far after each commercial for the benefit of the viewers who have just tuned in after abandoning another show. Advertisers create their displays in the full knowledge that most people will spend less than a second looking at them. Magazines charge more for advertising space on the back cover or on pages that will force the reader to pause, such as those pages that are made of stiffer, heavier paper, or those pages that fold out. Rock videos are created without narrative structure and with very rapid visual rhythms so that even a few seconds of viewing will produce high impact.

Mostly one look is all you get before you move on to something else, and media makers are competing fiercely, first to get you to give that one look to their product, and then to squeeze the most out of one look. Often a second look will betray the amount of respect the media makers had for their consumers in the constructing of their messages. Sometimes this conclusion is flattering of the consumer, and sometimes insulting.

Media education is all about taking that second look.

"Taking a second look" is more than simply looking at something more than once. If the second look is no different from the first one, it doesn't do much good. There are lots of people who have favorite videos, for instance, which they watch over and over again. But this doesn't necessarily qualify as taking a second look if all they see each time is the same they saw the first time. The media educator's definition of taking a second look includes seeing something new.

Such as: the flaw in the plot of the thriller movie which makes the ending impossible, or at least highly unlikely; the discrepancy between the news report on the radio and the same story reported in a newspaper; the scarcely hidden values messages that lurk within the stories, situations and characters that make up our entertainment telling us that it is OK to solve problems with violence, insults and guns, to act in ways that are demeaning to women, blacks, foreigners or minority groups; the fact that all the ads and articles in some women's magazine seem to be about grooming products and none of them about careers or work; the pictures in some ads which are clearly put together to be suggestive, evocative or startling to get attention or, by allusion, to capitalize on the familiarity of another picture or image; the newspaper which runs four editorials in a week on a single topic just before a favored candidate uses that same topic as a plank in an election platform.

Or such as: the realization that some magazines do not contain certain kinds of advertising, or that some magazines accept no advertising at all; the episodes of popular programs that deliberately contain strong, positive messages as if attempting to balance the violence and put-downs of the other shows; the movies that have hidden and rewarding depths; the newspapers that follow unpopular news stories; the books or stories that tap directly into the reader's

46

personal experience; the people who turn out to be more that they appeared to be at first acquaintance.

Sometimes, taking a second look means that you will deliberately seek out problems in media texts that make the world look simple. Propaganda, for instance, often paints a very rosy picture, and deliberately tries to lull the receiver into accepting the message uncritically. Consider, perhaps, a corporate TV ad promoting all the good works done by a certain trans-national lumber company. Maybe they actually do give scholarships and replant trees as the ad proclaims. But a viewer who takes a second look, seeking the problems in the deeper situation surrounding the ad will realize that the questions of polluted rivers, eroded mountainsides and exterminated wildlife are not even raised in the ad, let alone answered.

This technique of seeking out the problems in the larger context is called "problematizing'. Students who can problematize a media text are performing a very sophisticated kind of second-looking.

The ability to problematize is sometimes hard to turn off; it has the potential of becoming an orthodoxy. (See **ORTHODOXY IS THE ENEMY**) You will sometimes find that people are unable to read or watch a piece of media for enjoyment without pointing out all the things that it does not do. Most of the time these observations are accurate, but they are not always relevant, or wanted. For instance, problematizing an episode of *South Park* might not be a good idea if everyone else in the room is enjoying watching it. On the other hand, watching *South Park* regularly, without ever taking a second look or problematizing could be an approach more worthy of an ostrich than a student of media.

Of course, taking a second look is what media students have to do to analyze, deconstruct, appreciate, summarize, criticize, imitate, recommend or condemn any media text that comes their way. The problem, some of the time, is in convincing people to look again, to look beneath the surface, between the lines, inside the characters, through the image to find deeper and more rewarding levels of interpretation. English teachers have long known this, as they have struggled to engage students in the deep analysis of literature; media teachers have an advantage in that they are working with today's culture rather than yesterday's, but there is a danger in presenting media education in any way that makes the students feel their tastes are being put down.

YOUTH CRITICISM 101

"There are those, teacher and student alike, who bemoan their times a lost ... With long hair unkempt and bodies unwashed, they would put down the philosophy of their times and persuade all others with their constant denigrations and mournful fears.

They are sick and would inflict their sickness on all who would ignore or deride them."

As the author of this quotation shows, adults are prone to jump to negative conclusions about young people, and their cultural habits. For instance, we criticize them for their habit of surfing through the TV channels; watching two programs simultaneously; switching to a second channel when the commercials come on the first one; or using the picture-within-picture feature on the TV to see two shows at once. We complain if they start reading a book and then put it down, unfinished, or start another book before finishing the first one. We make superior clucking noises and put it all down to the short attention span of modern youth: their inability to concentrate; their need for Ritalin.

The invention of the digital radio tuner has made it possible for any teenager languishing on an unmade bed in an untidy room to zap a radio station at the press of a button, cutting from one tune to another without ever having to put up with the inconvenience of listening to commentary or commercials.

The dividing of newspapers into sections makes it easy for our teen (or our spouse) to go straight to the sports or the entertainment without ever having to look at anything we might personally call "news".

We might be missing the positive side of their behavior altogether. What if their avoidance of commercials were based on an awareness of their triviality, or on a genuine disinterest in commercialism? What if they really were capable of attending to more than one program at a time? What if they were merely imitating adult behavior in trying to keep pace with two or more sports events on a single weekend afternoon, and adapting it into an everyday thing?

What if their grab for the sports or the entertainment turned out to be nothing more than a clone of our own grab for the editorial or the business sections before dashing out of the house without breakfast?

What if their lack of attention and concentration were merely a reflection of living in a world of one-minute-managers, instant food, fast delivery and immediate feedback?

Is the one-minute manager, after all, a person who packs bursts of effectiveness into incredibly brief periods of time, or simply a person who can concentrate for any period of time up to sixty seconds? (That may be an unfair question. I think I know both kinds.)

I have a vivid memory of lecturing my high school student classes many years ago, in the PC (Pre Computer) era how it was impossible for an audio amplifier to respond to more than one signal at a time. I used to demonstrate by pointing out the different inputs on the back of amplifiers, and then indicating that the speakers could be fed only one of those signals at a time. My thesis was that the human brain was like an amplifier: capable of attending to only one input at a time. My point was that students should not play their record-players or radios when they were doing their homework.

Wrong.

The intention was good, and the logic quite reasonable, but the conclusion just was not in keeping with reality. My reasoning was based more on the moral superiority of adult assumptions than on the true evidence of human behavior. Our human brains are quite capable of attending to more than one input at a time, and even of using a second input to enhance the first, as we do with music in films. As I write this - on my PC in the PC (Post Computer) age - I am listening to the radio; I frequently read a book while watching TV; I am a living example of the folly of my earlier thesis. The kids knew it then. Some of the braver ones told me so.

If then I had thought about the technology of multiplexed radio signals, I would perhaps have been able to imagine that the human brain was as flexible as an FM transmitter or receiver.

SCREENING IMAGES

Another thing we criticize young people about is the evanescence of their media taste. "You spend $27 on a CD and play it for a week before throwing it on the heap of all the other CD's you've bought and used in the same way," I've ranted at my children One of them, with equanimity and aplomb, took the trouble to point out that I myself possess whole sets of CD's that I bought because of the bargain price, and which I have not yet removed from the plastic wrapper. Another showed me his collection of audio tapes, sampled from his favorite CD tracks, and also politely pointed out that I really had no idea how often he listened to his music, because I was rarely in his company when he had it on.

I tell these stories, not to elevate young people above adults, nor to ingratiate myself in the hope of achieving some of the youth that is by definition restricted to the young, but merely to remind myself, and perhaps some readers too, that adults sometimes jump to conclusions, and then sandbag those conclusions against the polite insistences of youth. In short, we are sometimes just plain wrong.

Here's one last example.

Picture the *paterfamilias* sitting in his countinghouse as the teenagers - duped and brainwashed by mindless commercials featuring braindead athletes - come home from a weekend foray into the mall, plastic bags in hand: evidence of yet more damage done to father's credit card.

"What, another pair of sneakers!? It's only a few weeks since you got the last pair." (and so on, with gestures.)

Kid runs up to bedroom with a sigh, thinking:

"Only last week you were on at me for wearing sneakers all the time, even in the snow, and now you wonder why they wear out. I can't win. You wear sneakers about ten times a year, and then brag that they last you for ever. Well, my dress shoes get worn about the same as your sneakers, and if I didn't keep growing out of them, they'd last as long."

By the way, the quotation that leads off this chapter is from a famous Chinese writer and philosopher. His name was Confucius, and he wrote this about 2500 years ago.

Ageism, I think they call it. Ageism isn't very PC.

TEACHING MEDIA ON THE CHEAP

The problems most often mentioned as preventing teachers from teaching the media in their classrooms are: lack of training, and lack of equipment and budget. My belief is that neither one needs to be a very formidable obstacle.

As for lack of training, we all know a lot about media, teacher and student alike. The knowledge may not be very well organized into theory, but it's there nevertheless. We all know how we're supposed to feel in response to various kinds of background music in movies. We all know how to find different kinds of information in a newspaper. We can all (almost) tell the difference between the articles and the ads in a magazine. We may not, however, have spent much time thinking about and describing these different kinds of knowledge.

In a classroom where media education is an exploration and an inquiry, it's OK for teachers and students to be exploring together. The traditional assumptions about teachers being in the know while the students are in the dark, often have more to do with power relationships in the classroom than with learning. A teacher who understands learning and inquiry approaches can be quite at ease in the media classroom, even without formal training in media education.

What can we do in the media education classroom with limited budget? Here are a few suggestions.

First, find out where the budget control is, and start to compete with all the other school priorities for a fair budget for media education. Do your homework by gathering details of the kinds of expenditures you think are reasonable. Write a well developed budget rationale, connected to your program objectives, and submit it to your school principal. If your budget request is turned down, ask for a commitment for budget in another year. Try to get some long term commitment, so that you can plan your media program on more than an ad hoc basis.

If your budget for buying newspapers for classroom study doesn't run to the expense of buying class sets of papers every day, take heart. Yesterday's newspapers are free! All you have to do is to organize a number of students and teachers to bring their yesterday's newspaper into school each day. This will provide you with several copies of the same newspapers each day. It may be necessary to survey several classes to get all the papers you need. In some ways it's better to be looking at day-old newspapers. Perceptions of news reporting are sometimes easier to access when our perspective of the story itself is not muddied by novelty. Be sure to arrange for a recycling program to look after all the newsprint after your classes have finished with the papers.

In the same way that old newspapers are free, so are old magazines. It's a good practice in the media classroom to set up a regular drop-off point for back issues of all kinds of magazines, flyers and catalogs. This resource will be infinitely useful: for the formal and comparative study of styles and organizations of different kinds of magazines; as a source of visual material for students to use in making photo-montages, collages, illustrated reports, story boards, animation boards, mock-ups of new magazine formats; as source material for the study of print media advertising; as source material for the study of journalistic style.

If video cameras, movie cameras and editing facilities are not available, consider using some or all of the following: tell a visual story using 35mm slides, or prints, or Polaroid shots; tell a visual story using only a story-treatment (outline) and story board; tell a visual story using only visual material "found" in other sources, such as magazines; tell a visual story using comic book format and style; substitute a radio report or story for the visual, and use audio tape which can be edited easily and cheaply.

Students can learn a great deal about animation, 16mm film and its operation by doing exercises drawing on blank 16mm film, or scratching on black film. Overhead projector markers or India ink are ideal for the drawing medium, and the 16mm film stock can usually be obtained almost free by: picking up old 16mm films in garage sales;

getting discarded films from your local school board library or public library; visiting film laboratories or TV stations and asking for any discarded film. In order to remove the emulsion from film to make it clear, soak it in a warm solution of chlorine bleach, and then scrape, wipe or scrub the emulsion off. Be sure to observe safety regulation when you use chlorine bleach. A few trials will help you establish the best water temperature, level of bleach concentration and time of soaking.

Garage sales can provide you with many items for your media classroom: look for old magazines for your classroom archive; a/v equipment such as slide or filmstrip projectors; open reel tape recorders; super 8mm film cameras, projectors and editing equipment; copies of old 16mm films for your animation workshop; old records; old computers that could be useful, even if only for the use of the monitor. A grub stake for buying at garage sales might be available from your PTA or your students' council.

Your public library may have a collection of video or 16mm films that you can borrow free for classroom use. The NFB in some areas also operates a video library, and programs that you want to use regularly are for sale cheap. Talk to your school librarian about acquiring some titles for your own school. Some provinces offer a wealth of TV material for use in schools through their educational TV network.

Divert students' attention from TV to radio. Portable cassette tape recorders are easily available in schools and homes. Tapes are plentiful and cheap. To edit audio tape, though, you have to have an open reel tape deck. But even these can usually be found for next to nothing. In many schools it's only a question of finding the cupboard where the old open reel tape recorders are hidden. First of all, ask the modern language teachers. If your school is more than 25 years old, it's likely that the French or Spanish teachers have an open reel recorder that they used with old French instructional programs. When the programs were replaced, the tape recorders frequently were shelved and forgotten.

If the copyright law and the cost of video for schools is prohibiting the use of video in your classroom, consider taking the monitor into your classroom and basing your TV study on the material that is available on air during your class time. In most parts of the

SCREENING IMAGES

country, and at different times of the day, you'll be able to find pretty well every kind of TV programming that you'd want to use in class.

Cable in the Classroom, CNN, CBC Newsworld, and many others offer a wealth of copyright- and commercial-free school programming. There's no need to put your students in thrall to YNN or Channel One to get access to good materials.

So you haven't got access to a sophisticated desk-top publishing program. Then compile the newspaper pages that your students create from Letraset, type-written or word-processed print-outs, by pasting them up on oversized newsprint blue sheets or on a bulletin board. If you have access to a reducing/magnifying photo-copying machine, you may be able to develop some different sized fonts quite cheaply.

If it's important for you to study night-time TV programming in class, and yet the copyright law prevents you from using those programs, make the viewing a homework assignment, and use the class time for the follow-up work.

Consider making a classroom study of mass media which are already part of the students' own possessions. For instance, have students bring in samples of media such as: postage stamps, baseball/hockey/etc cards, buttons, printed T-shirts, fashion, toys, packaging, junk mail - and use these as a basis of a mass media study.

MEDIA LITERACY ACROSS THE CURRICULUM

(This chapter is adapted from a speech given at a symposium of high school history teachers.)

Let's take a look at some of the different kinds of media we have in our classrooms, ask ourselves how we use them and if we are using them to their potential.

We use fashion: clothing, accessories, make up: all the mass produced paraphernalia that change our appearance and communicate to others certain messages about ourselves. This doesn't necessarily apply only to students and their gear that brands them as prep, or punk. It applies to the teachers whose corduroy or silk carries a message, too. But we don't always consciously use it. We are sometimes unconsciously part of it.

We use the informal, perhaps daily, discussion in class on current events, which is really an informal discussion about the version of current events we have received through our news media that day or the day before. How often does that discussion venture into the realm of actually questioning the sources or the channels of the information? How often does it make the tacit assumption that the news reports were factual and accurate?

There's the mass medium of the text book, which sometimes dominates the information flow within a classroom. How often do teachers encourage students to question the processes that dictate the formation of textbooks? How aware are we as teachers of the ways that decisions get made within publishing houses? Who is in charge of the curriculum? If it is the publishers, which division of the publishers has the biggest influence? Design? Editing? Marketing? What pressure groups try to influence publishers? What kinds of influence do they try to have?

In schools we tend to rely heavily on the medium of print. We tend to invest in print a kind of respectability that we do not grant to any other medium. We have a strong preference for a kind of print that uses forms of language peculiar to our world of education and academia. In other words, if it isn't in a book, we don't believe it. And if a kid doesn't put it in an essay, we don't give it marks.

I argue that we should use media more in our classrooms by encouraging students to report to us in radio documentary formats, in video tape presentations, in magazine layouts, advertising campaign proposals, in song and music. It's not that I think we need to bring media into our classrooms to increase the incidence of couch potatoness among our students. I don't really advocate that history teachers should look for Hollywood feature films that will sugar coat the pill of the 100 years war, or Robin Hood, unless the topic they are investigating is how we receive historical information, and how the channels of communication affect our perceptions of what history really is. A few hours spent watching the History Channel would illustrate this point. The question should be a part of every history course.

If we bring media into our classrooms, then we are subjecting students to versions of information that have been edited and modified by those who control those media. In the medium of education, by the way, it is frequently the teachers who manipulate the information, and re-version it into something else.

The purpose of the media in our own society is to make money. Media are commercial enterprises, and sooner or later they are going to end up compromising fine ideals for commercial reasons.

Media in totalitarian societies are controlled by the government and exist to pass on the government's messages. Totalitarian societies call their own alternative media subversive, and they suppress them by withholding official permission or by police action. They call our alternative or underground media "democratic". In our society, we call our underground media pinko, and suppress them by withholding advertising or public funding. We call the totalitarian alternative media "freedom loving".

When we ask if we are using media to their potential in the classroom, the question supposes that we are in the position of making the decisions about the influence of the media on our classrooms.

Ideas for Media Education

There is, perhaps, a suggestion that the media will only influence our classrooms if we deliberately bring them into the room ourselves, and show videos, films, slides, play tapes, read magazines and newspapers right there in the class. This is of course, absolute folly. The media are constantly affecting the whole world and all its institutions, including education, and if the world doesn't put part of its energy into understanding the influences of media, then there is a danger that influence will become control.

In all societies, the act of attempting to obtain free and unlimited access to honest and full sources of information is called an attack on "national security". (Oliver North goes free when the alternative is to reveal to the public what actually was going on.) In times of war, even in our society, people who point out that the populace is being fed a controlled diet of half truths by those who control the media, could find themselves behind bars, or worse.

Here are some questions all teachers should ask about media and their influence in all classrooms:

- Do we use media, or do we willingly submit to its use of us?
- Are the media the handmaidens of society, or is our culture the product of mass media conditioning?
- Has there ever been a time when the populace was not manipulated by an elite group for its own ends?
- Do the mass media and their ability to pass along huge amounts of information, actually put modern generations in a better position than the medieval serfs when it comes to the ability to control one's own destiny, and to influence the course of events?
- What would have been the reaction in 12th century Europe if we had asked," are we using the full potential of the feudal system in our classrooms?"

MEDIA LITERACY

In a world where the media are blamed for half of the ills of humankind, from rampant consumerism to crime, sex, violence and rock 'n roll, I fear the disappointment that will inevitably follow the discovery that a "media literate" populace does not change its media ways. It's too simple a formula to think that changing the level of knowledge about media in a technologically sophisticated society, or that changing the media themselves will have much influence on the values that underlie the behavior of that society's citizens.

In assessing how children react to media, I turn to the theories of personal response to literature; and in assessing how children make media, I look for models that allow student product to be evaluated or assessed by the audience it was intended for. (See my book, *ASSESSING MEDIA WORK: Authentic Assessment in Media Education,* Wright Communications, 1996.)

It would be a mistake, I believe, to break media education down in to bits and pieces like sound, shape, color and movement, and to try to teach these bits in sequence as a curriculum. I'm thinking about how ability to write is sometimes confused with ability to spell accurately and to follow certain arbitrary and arcane rules of usage that are frequently mistaken for grammar. I'd hate to see media education systematized and institutionalized and scientized into a set of basics that had to be mastered before kids were allowed to watch TV.

Don't misunderstand me. I am interested in rigor. I do believe in scholarship. I am concerned about the level of communicative disability (or is it disinclination?) that seems to pervade or society. It's just that I believe the solutions to educational problems lie in learning rather than in instruction, and that individuals learn to be good communicators in direct proportion to the amount of real opportunities they have to communicate. Good writers do lots of writing. Good readers got to be good at reading by practicing: by practicing reading, not by doing work sheets.

In this sense, or society contains very few citizens who are not practiced in the literacy of media. Adults know how to make the newspaper or a magazine serve many uses. Children know how to use TV for learning, for entertainment, to kill time, or just to keep away the bogeyman. Adolescents have mastered dozens of uses for movies in theatres. All of these people developed all of these abilities in using the media without the benefit of any formal instruction. They didn't even use mail-order courses. They learned by doing.

We have seen this time and again in children. We have watched infants discover the need to talk, and we have not been able to comprehend the speed of their learning language. We have witnessed children discover the power and joy of being able to read, and have been scarcely able to keep up with the demand for more books. We have known adults who stumbled unwillingly into word processing, suddenly discovered what it could do for them, and watched amazed as they taught themselves the mysteries of keyboarding, and problem-solved their way through software manuals that might as well otherwise be written in a foreign language. There is no denying that human learning is based on personally perceived need.

Students will become able in the media when they are given lots of chances to work in the media; when schools expect to see students report about what they have learned in all subject areas using all the media.

Instead of asking always for an essay, teachers could consider the following 186 alternative formats for student reporting. The media are part of all learning.

SCREENING IMAGES

abstract
ad campaign
adaptation
address
advertisement
animation
announcement
anthology
autobiography
bibliography
bill board
biography
brainstorming
brochure
calculation
campaign
caption
cartoon
cartoon strip
character sketch
chart
collage
column
commercial
costume
crossword
cut-line
debate
dedication
definition
demonstration
design
desk-top
   publishing
diagram
dialogue
diary
diorama
directions
directive
discussion

display
docudrama
drama
drawing
editorial
electronic mail
epigram
epitaph
ESSAY
eulogy
executive
summary
fashion design
fiction
film
filmography
foreword
game
graffiti
graph
greeting card
guest speaker
guidebook
guidelines
handbill
handbook
headline
horoscope
how-to guide
improvisation
inscription
instructions
interpretation
interview
introduction
invitation
invoice
job description
joke
journal article
journal

label
lecture
letter to the
   editor
letter
list
log
magazine
manual
map
memoir
memorandum
menu
message
mime
minutes
model
monologue
music
news report
news article
newsletter
newspaper
note making
note taking
one-sheet
organizer
painting
pamphlet
parable
paragraph
paraphrase
periodical
photo-montage
photograph
play
plot diagram
poem
postcard
poster
précis

Ideas for Media Education

preface
problem solving
profile
project
prologue
proposal
prospectus
publishing
puppetry
puzzle
query
quest
question list
question
questionnaire
quiz
quotation
radio report
receipt
recipe
report
research paper
resource list
resume
review
riddle
role-play
routing slip
saying
scenario
script
semantic
  organizer
sign
simulation
skit
slogan
sociogram
song

speech
statement
story board
story-telling
story-writing
summary
survey
table
tableau
telegram
test
title
transformation
travelogue
treatment
trip
uniform
video
visit
visitor
viva voce
waybill
word search
word-web

ELECTIONS AS MEDIA EDUCATION

Elections are blessings without disguise for media students of all ages. It is during elections that some of the hoariest old tricks of the media trade are trotted out in the attempt to sway the opinions of the mass, with several years of political power as the prize for the winner. Voters and voters-in-training, can cast their ballots far more intelligently if they do so with full knowledge of how the media have tried to sway their opinions. Nothing is more precious than the right to make up your own mind, and we are constantly on the edge of seeing a display of the latest as well as the oldest techniques that have been thought up to relieve us of the tedious necessity of exercising that right. The next election, like Christmas, is always just around the corner.

Here are some ways you could approach the topic through media education:

Start right away to collect every issue of every paper you can get your hands on. Hoard copies of magazines, and treasure the ones you can find from other countries with commentary on the election.

Organize some grand scale scrap-book-keeping, either by candidate, by party, or by publication. Add your own marginal notes as often as you can.

Keeping video files and radio files is more complex than keeping print files, but it will be very rewarding. You might want to specialize in keeping only files of a certain newscast day-over-day; or you might want to collect campaign ads for scrutiny

Another way is to have different people keep diaries on the coverage of different TV and radio stations and networks. Don't ignore some of the least likely candidates such as the cable music and "education" channels.

Seize the opportunity to have some serious talks to make sure you understand topics such as:

- the differences among facts, conclusions, interpretations, opinions, myths and prejudices
- the importance of photo-ops and sound bites, and the effect these have on serious reporting
- the way individual newspapers, or networks select a party to favor, and then slant their coverage of the campaign to give the advantage to candidates for that party
- how the corporate interests of the media source (TV network, newspaper) might influence the interpretation of the story
- how the study of content analysis, discourse analysis and body language can reveal what kinds of opinions and intentions the candidates really have, and how those might differ from what they claim in their words

Compile the various predictions of the pollsters and pundits, and examine them for variety, consistency, bias and reliability.

Collect political cartoons and cartoon strips and talk about them to see how politics influences the media and how the media influence politics.

Perform column-inch counts in various papers to find which parties/candidates receive the most (prominent) coverage. Compare these findings to the editorial policies of the newspapers to seek further insights.

Keep a watch on humor and scandal-mongering. Which comedians indulge in partisan political jiggery-jokery? What jokes are doing the rounds about the various candidates, and what prejudices do the jokes reveal? Which late-night comedy shows favor one candidate and which favor another. Talk about how you can tell.

Keep track of all the celebrity endorsements, both stated and implied, that are included in your daily media diet as an attempt to influence your decision of how to vote.

Talk about the general attitude taken by the candidates and/or the media to the intelligence of the average voter. How many babies are kissed? hot-dogs eaten? ribbons cut? trees planted? Foundation stones laid? What does any of this have to do with politics?

Keep a count of all the promises and policies announced by each of the major party leaders. Note date and location for each one. At the end of the campaign write a tally of them all and send each leader a copy of your work with an appropriate letter outlining your expectations of a party leader in view of all those promises and policies.

Periodically write again to each leader with a reminder of the status of each policy statement or promise and ask for specific answers to questions based upon your perception of the leaders' performance on those same promises and policies.

Explore some of the following "what if?" scenarios :

- What if voters decided to cast their votes depending on the best showing of the candidates in their own constituencies, instead of voting on party lines?
- What if the media were to concentrate on showing the candidates as they are, instead of trying to make one appear better than the others, or of picking on one symbolic image? (Pierre Trudeau extending the finger, Gerald Ford returning the meal to his host.)
- What if the voters decided to ignore all the blatant manipulation of the campaign and vote according to the issues and the positions taken by the candidates?
- What if one of the TV networks opted out from the daily photo-op and sound-bite game of the leaders' cross country tours, and concentrated solely on issues and policies?

It may appear that I am recommending that you get involved in a lot of time-consuming stuff, that you really can't afford to do. Fair enough. Yet I ask to you to analyze the situation briefly and ask yourself this question: "When am I asked to make a decision that could have and a bigger and more wide-ranging effect upon my life and the lives of all citizens, than when I am asked to make up my mind in an election?"

You may decide it's worth the time and effort after all.

NEGOTIATING MEANING

On my drive home from work, there's a certain radio station I like to listen to. It has intelligent interviews; it has items on the arts; it plays music; it warns you about traffic tie-ups, and it doesn't have any commercials. But, at a certain time each afternoon, it plays a piece of country and western music, and if there's one kind of music that I dislike, it's C & W. And so I find myself switching to another station almost every day, to avoid listening to a kind of music that I don`t like.

I've watched my children picking a program to watch on TV clutching the zapper in their hand. (In my sister's house, they call it "the stick". Nobody seems to have a positive name for this instrument.) My children seem to spend less than a second on each station before making up their mind to move on to the next. They're faster at changing channels than I am at avoiding C & W.

I was working recently with a writing team in my own board of education. We were talking about the concept of how we approach media messages: how we tend either to accept, reject or Negotiate the media messages that are offered to us. It was the word "Negotiate" that was causing the most trouble. We agreed that we often accept or reject some media messages, but we weren't quite sure that we agreed on how we enter into negotiation with a media text.

Negotiating with a text is not always as simple as changing one's mind from positive to negative or the reverse. Sometimes we find that a media text presents problems. In order to solve these problems, we enter into a different kind of relationship with the text. We may try to look at it again. We may seek out someone to talk to about it. We may try to find something written about it, either in a newspaper review or in a critical periodical. We talk about films being "difficult"; we talk about how hard we had to work to understand a TV drama. We deliberately become more active in our involvement with the text. Acceptance and rejection can come out of passive response,

SCREENING IMAGES

but negotiation is more active. (See **SEASONAL LESSONS IN MEDIA EDUCATION**)

This strikes me as one of the areas in media study that could be very fruitful for teachers and students to explore together as a genuine inquiry. I'd like to share some musings of my own on the topic, taken from my personal journal.

I'm sitting in the hotel room watching rock videos. I'm trying to figure them out and I'm beginning to feel that some of them are structured deliberately to prevent me from succeeding. They seem to be made so that they will be perpetually challenging. Am I paranoid? My experience with them - my attempts at responding and interpreting - are constantly frustrated by the speed of everything. The cuts are so fast. The style changes so quickly. The shots have so little to link them together. The narrative is so obscure and shifting. So many of the shots seem intended only to create an impression rather than to transmit information or to connect logically to something else. I'm concluding that the maximum response expected is at the knee-jerk level. They seem to come as close as they dare to pornography. I'm very much aware of my reaction's root in masculine middle age.

I'm thinking about this. I'm beginning to apply critical analysis to my own reactions, and to question whether the world of rock videos is as bad as I first think. Creeping in from the edges of my memories are images from art and experimental films that have challenged and puzzled me in recent years. Comparisons of technique between them and these slick expensive videos, create more new questions rather than answers. Why is it that this TV format is the spawning ground for new mainstream techniques? Are we wrong, perhaps, to think of rock video as a new format? Are videos merely commercials for the music business? If so, then Pauline Kael's belief that the advertising industry "incorporates" innovation will explain it.

I know that rock videos have already had tremendous effect on mainstream TV and film. I remember *Max Headroom, Miami Vice,* and Richard Lester. (Where are they now?)

When I apply feminist principles to videos, I come up with all kinds of problems. Why is it that even the women's musical groups sell themselves as sex objects? How have women allowed themselves to be co-opted into the iconography of male sexual fantasy? My critical awareness oscillates between conditioned male response and intellectual feminist awareness, and the result is very uncomfortable. I am at the same time attracted to these images of female bodies and critical of the way that they are being served up to me for commercial gain. In the middle of this oscillation is a kind of awareness of the technological cleverness of it all. I think, all in all, I'm eager to end up in a neutral, negotiated position with these texts. I'm very fearful of the position which puts me in the camp of either total acceptance or total rejection. Perhaps my intellectualizing is a form of escape.

The question is: how do we as teachers encourage young people to seek that same, considered middle ground between uncritical acceptance and rejection of text? And how do we develop in our students some kind of awareness of their own perception?

OUR MEDIA DEFINE US

In many ways, we can define ourselves by the media that we consume. We know a lot about people when we know which newspapers they buy, which TV programs are their favorites, what kind of music they prefer, where they buy their clothes, what is their radio station of choice, and so on. In a nostalgic moment recently, (and after looking again at Michael Apted's wonderful documentaries, *28UP, 35 UP,* and *42 UP*) it came to me that our media memories contribute a lot towards our understanding of ourselves as well. An important part of all education, and particularly of media education, is the process of growing in self-understanding.

For instance, I have often been on the verge of criticizing my teenage son for renting so many movies at the video store, (and for renting what to me is not worth watching) when I have remembered my own teenage years when I went to the movies a regular five times a week, and went to see anything that was playing, regardless.

I have inwardly groaned as my daughter picked up yet another *Sweet Valley High* book, and had to bite my tongue by remembering for how many years I was a passionate and indiscriminate consumer of books by Enid Blyton, and later, Capt. W. E. Johns.

Likewise, I have had to remember some of the outlandish clothes I wore as an undergraduate, and some of the defiant haircuts I've sported at all times of my life, to prevent myself from commenting on similar behavior in young people close to me.

People seem to find aspects of themselves in various components of mass media, and then adopt those media as expressions of themselves. And I see no harm in it.

Ideas for Media Education

What I insist is important, though, is some form of critical awareness to accompany this adoption of media as expression. I do not want to criticize the kids who (un)dress like Madonna, but I would like them to be able to express in fairly cogent terms why they want to do so. If the answer comes out in terms of how neat it is to upset adults with teenage behavior, then I think that is a good explanation, provided it is offered only once and not habitually, as some sort of a cop out. I may not like it as an explanation, but I think that it is truthful, logical and indicative of some thought process other than blind imitation. I would prefer that the answer went into more detail, but as an opener, it would suit me.

And the sort of detail that I would be delighted to have students explore is stuff like:

- what kinds of interests the student has that connect with the media text
- what it is in the personalities or the lives of the individuals connected to the text that is attractive to the student
- how the representation in the text connects with the experience/the hopes/the fears of the student
- what other activity that is attractive to the student is connected to this representation
- what qualities in the text are seen by the student as being good, and why they are better represented here than in other texts

I was making pancakes for the family brunch the other Sunday, (you know, the way men do) when I had one of those funny deja vu sort of experiences that took me back to my childhood. I grew up during WW II in England, and there were many experiences that I had never had because of all the shortages. One of these experiences was to taste a pancake. I guess you needed Eggs and butter for pancakes, and they were pretty hard to get. Anyway, I was a good five years old before I saw my mother cook a pancake, and that was probably on some Shrove Tuesday soon after the end of the war, Shrove Tuesday being known in Britain as "pancake day".

Now even though I had never had a pancake, I knew that what you were supposed to do with them was to toss them up in the air and have them land back in the pan the other side up. I realized on that Sunday morning at brunch that the place where I got that knowledge about pancakes was from all the picture comic books that I read during the war, in which the heroes never suffered from any of the shortages that afflicted the general population. I realized also that I was more concerned about seeing the pancake tossed, than I was about actually eating it.

In just the same way, I came to know all about bananas. My picture comic books educated me in all the intricacies of bananadom. I knew how banana peels were good for putting on sidewalks in just the right places at the right time; I knew how you were supposed to hold a banana ready to strip the peel off; I knew how to eat a banana with half the peel draped over your fist. All this I knew because I had seen it in my comics, and, I suppose in the movies that my parents took me to. But I had never actually seen a real banana until I was about six years old. When I finally did get one, my grandmother, not understanding that it was the very experience of peeling the thing that I was hankering after, and not the taste of it, kindly peeled and sliced it for me. I cried for a long time over that.

I guess I've known for some time that there's more money to be made in advertising the sizzle than the steak, but I hadn't quite noted before how far-reaching that concept could be. Do children today get disappointed if their first pizza isn't thrown up into the air by a cook in a chef's hat? Is the current concept of designer clothing preference another manifestation of the same thing? Is the annual Christmas let down another? When was it that brewers realized they could sell more beer by advertising the attributes of beer consumption rather than by stressing the qualities of the beer itself?

Later I started thinking about other, more adult experiences I've had.

Back in the days when fathers were assiduously kept out of delivery rooms, I found myself in a solitary waiting room in a maternity wing. This had never happened to me before, and so I really had no personal experience to fall back on to tell me how to behave. Where did I find the model for my behavior then? You guessed it: from the movies; from TV; from stories and novels. In short, from my media experience.

Somehow that day, my mind was filled with images of myself unshaven, with jacket off, necktie askew, shirt wrinkled, pacing up and down in the waiting room, wearing a track on the carpet, filling the ash trays with half finished cigarettes, littering the floor with crumpled paper coffee cups, frantically grabbing every person who entered the room by the collar and demanding news. The fact that I didn't really want to behave in any of these ways, but really wanted to go to sleep, made me feel guilty at first. But that feeling did pass when I realized how foolish I felt when I actually tried to match the stereotype for a while by doing the pacing.

I wonder how many more of our behaviors are modelled for us in advance of our having a need for them, to the point where we actually feel an obligation to follow them. I wonder if the media actually do construct mythologies for us.

WATCHING HOW YOU WATCH TV

One of the advantages - or one of the curses - of having cable or satellite television access is that you can nearly always find something on some channel that is to your liking. Time was when we had the choice of two or three networks and that was all. Many of us remember one - with rabbit ears, black and white. If you didn't like what was on, you were out of luck. Read a book; take a walk; don't tell me your problems.

Of course, having much more choice will make it far less tempting for us ever to read a book or take a walk, or tell people our problems. And that itself could be a massive problem for us each to solve individually. We are faced day after day and evening after evening with a tempting array of programs on an ever expanding series of channels some of which are tailored exactly to our tastes - or prejudices.

The classic movie channel, for instance, may not be everybody's cup of tea, but for the likes of me it could be a drug, a potential addiction. Others could be affected the same way by the country music channel, or the home-shopping channel. Matter of fact, I know people in each of those obsessive categories. Twenty four hours a day of just what you're looking for, and never any need to go seeking anything else.

The trend has a number of different names. Some call it niche marketing, others call it narrowcasting. Whatever its name, we're going to get lots more of it. Why? Just like Everest, because it's there; and because we can; and because people can prove that it's good at selling stuff: either widgets or values. Imagine some of the channels that could be available:

Ideas for Media Education

- a yo-yo channel
- an embroidery channel
- a Holocaust denial channel
- a window replacement channel
- an anarchist channel (no schedule available)

Hell in a hand basket. That's where some people say we're headed. And lots of them want to put the blame squarely on the shoulders of TV. They want us to believe that TV is causing all the rotten things in the world to happen. Teens get pregnant because of TV. (Go figure.) People get hooked on drugs because of TV. Families fall apart because of TV. People are violent because of TV. People can't read because of TV.

And the way to fix it all is to fix TV. Stop the violence on TV and watch the people all of a sudden get gentle (like Barney?) Censor the content of TV programs and see people suddenly start being nice to each other. Put a stop to the drug trade by saturating the airwaves with public service announcements (PSAs) on clean living. Drive the condom manufacturers into bankruptcy by programming chastity stories wall to wall.

Some of this may even work a little bit. But not to the extent some people are betting. It's all too easy. Putting all the blame on TV makes a good sound-bite, but omits huge parts of the issues. It pays no attention to the personal context, the psychological context and - most of all - the social context.

Far better for each of us, or for each group of us to take responsibility for our own viewing and for the results of it. Far better for us to pay as much attention to the way we watch TV as we do to the purchase of a book, or the selection of a vacation.

By now, my family is used to watching my strange behavior at the Saturday breakfast table. Here's what I do. After the food, I sit back with my second cup of tea - made with boiling water, steeped for 3 1/2 minutes, milk (not cream) in the cup first, half a teaspoon of sugar, please - grab a highlighter pen, and settle down with the Toronto Star TV Magazine.

First, I read the section called "TV Worth Watching" to see if there's anything listed there that I should try to see. It mentions not only regular series and specials, but documentaries and sports events, too. To my chagrin, it also recommends programs on channels that I don't subscribe to, so sometimes I am left wishing. However, we decided long ago in my family that our cable bill was already high enough - no more new channels.

Next, I look through the page of movie recommendations, before I check out the entire week's movie listings. Like a player in a smoky Bingo palace, I dab all the programs I want to see, both in the articles I read and then later in the daily schedules.

Finally, I go through the daily listings to see if the series that I try to follow are showing new episodes or repeats. If there are new episodes, I dab them, too.

What emerges from this process is a TV magazine of many colors, but one that customizes my potential TV viewing for the week. It's far more efficient than if I relied on the technique of sitting down on the sofa whenever the inclination took me to zap through twenty or so channels on what my father, a die-hard movie fan, always referred to as "the idiot's lantern."

Some days, I end up with nothing marked at all. Other days I have an absolute traffic jam of programs to see, all overlapping with each other. You know Murphy's law of TV scheduling: "If in any week there are only three things worth watching on TV, then those three things shall be scheduled on the same night at the same time." (Poor Murphy, why do we blame it all on him?)

But this is where the VCR comes in handy. I can not tell a lie, I use two of them. More family amusement ensues when on some evenings, I dash about the house with video tapes to record two programs on tape while I watch a third. Epithets such as "couch potato" have been known to be uttered at such times. (Is this, like the reference to Murphy, another slur against the Irish?) Also, some family negotiating takes place when my three choices conflict with the choices of other family members. Needless to say, I don't always have my way.

Yet, I maintain that my way of approaching TV is saner than most. I plan. And then I follow my plan. A lot of what I see is time-shifted by the VCR. I skip through the commercials, and sometimes, end up skipping the program, too, because it turns out to be less than I expected. (Or because I made a mistake and recorded the wrong show.) In those cases, though, I usually have another tape standing by, so I don't have to resort to surfing channels, looking for any eye-candy that attracts my attention.

I reckon the way I use technology is better than the way contemplated by those who hail the V Chip as our savior from TV nastiness. I'm not prepared to allow a V Chip to determine what is fit to watch and what is not. So long as I have my own faculties intact, (some members of my family have been known to claim that time has already passed) I will make up my own mind. V Chips are likely to favor the sickly sweet, the inoffensive, the blandly peaceful, the sort of video Soma that will put the populace to sleep so that the economic and political sub-text of TV can exploit them all the more. Challenging, thoughtful or merely controversial material will get caught in the electronic leg-hold because it might contain a little sex, violence, or profanity.

Spicy, challenging and stimulating programs like *NYPD Blue* will be driven to the borders of respectability, while porridge like *The Disney Hour* will get served up time after time. I would hate to be forced to choose perpetually between *The Disney Hour* or its equivalents because they measured down to the levels of tolerance programmed into a computer chip in my TV.

No. You should take hold of your own TV viewing. Get rid of the remote control. Never sit in front of the TV without a purpose. Move the TV into a location where going to watch it is an effort rather than a whimsy. Make your own decisions.

If you were to compare TV consumption with food consumption, you would be looking to curb TV gluttony. You would be wise, though, to remember that with food, there is an opposite to gluttony, called anorexia.

What is it, then, that families want to protect children from?

- Is it just that people think children spend too much of their time in front of TV sets, so that they have less time for other important childhood activities like playing outdoors, reading, hobbies and sports? Well, that is part of the answer, but it is not the entire source of people's anxiety.

- Is it that adults are anxious that children should not be exposed to some of the programs that they believe are good, but not suitable for children? Yes, this too is part of the answer, but not all of it.

- Is it that parents are concerned about the commercialism that pervades TV, where children are bombarded with ads to buy, or to get someone else to buy products that are not needed? This is often a big part of the anxiety, but once again it is not the whole story.

- Is it that TV has a reputation for showing stories that include violence, sex, drug-use, and disrespect for race, gender, class, faith, sexual orientation and disability which together might skew the children's perception of the world and eventually their behavior? Bingo.

This last reason is the big one in many people's minds. Most people are reasonable about "sensitive issues", (See: **VIOLENCE, SEX, DRUGS, AND -ISMS IN THE MEDIA**) They realize there is no one-to-one relationship between seeing and doing. Watching violence does not automatically make people violent. But most people, too, are concerned, and want to do something constructive about TV habits in their own families.

These people believe a moderate exposure to sensitive issues in TV and other media is not going to do them, or probably their children, any harm. They worry, though, about too much. Too much might fatten and soften the brain the way too much food fattens and softens the body. Lots of people think it can sicken the brain, too.

How much is too much might depend on how much you are prepared to exercise your brain. If your brain is totally inactive, sedentary, in neutral, permanently out of critical mode, then you may be a good candidate for some ill effects from TV. But a healthy, active brain can shake off many threatened ill effects and grow stronger on the same TV diet that may make others sick. This fact offers up a challenging dilemma for those who would censor TV for fear of its possible ill effects.

Here's what you can do:

- **Be selective**: Instead of just flopping down on the couch with the remote in your hand, plan your TV viewing in advance. It's the couch potato who ends up watching whatever is on, and wondering at the end of the evening where all the time went. The idea is to watch nothing without a good reason. (Sometimes, "I'm tired, and I need a break." is an excellent reason.)
- **Use the technology wisely**: use your VCR to record programs from one time slot so that you can watch them at a more convenient time. To do this you will have to know how to program your VCR. If this is a problem, ask your teenagers to show you how. If you don't have a teenager, consider renting one from a neighbor.

Watching time shifted TV is very effective in a number of ways:

- You watch the show when you want to
- You can fast forward through the parts that are not to your liking

- If you decide not to watch it, you can go straight on to the next tape, without having to kill time waiting for the new program to come up.
- It is something you have planned, and therefore will take more seriously than something that just popped up
- You can fast-forward through the commercials, saving time and cutting down on your exposure to ads.

Some technologies like the V Chip might end up being a snare and a delusion, if people use them as an excuse for not thinking or doing anything other than trying to shut the door on some programs they think they would not like. Also, producers might use the V Chip as an excuse to pass all responsibility for TV content to the consumer. They might load up their programs with even more sensationalism, and say, "You don't have to watch it if you don't like it."

Better to watch something that could be disturbing and spend time talking about it than to allow the technology to keep it from your eyes. The V Chip could end up being bad for TV consumers: a surprise that works to narrow the mind by limiting the options, that constricts understanding instead of broadening it.

- **Don't fall for eye-candy all the time**: skipping channels with the zapper is setting yourself up for junk TV. You'll end up browsing on eye-candy, grazing instead of satisfying yourself. Turning TV into a perpetual sampler with no whole pieces anywhere. One of the most important things you need to include in your TV diet is wholes. Not fragments, but things that are complete in themselves. Whole documentaries; complete, in-depth news reports; thoughtful comedies; challenging dramas. Fragments pass by your eyes but never engage your critical thinking. You might even get addicted to not being challenged. Wholes work more slowly, challenging you to think, assess and make conclusions, perhaps to discuss, dispute or argue. Fragments may flit past the mind, wholes are more likely to stimulate it.
- **Allow yourself some indulgences**: TV is, after all, an entertainment medium, and you are entitled to some mindless entertainment. The trick is to know when you need it, and to enjoy it without guilt. Make TV your servant, not your controller. Pick what you want, and know what you need.

SCREENING IMAGES

- **Allow for personal preferences**: when you are making your TV menu, you've got to make allowances for people's foibles. In my family, father (that's me) refuses to watch horror shows. He just plain doesn't like to be scared. Mother is not too taken with sports. And daughter can't stand what she calls "high-fallutin' artsy stuff". No problem, a little family give-and-take makes this easy to solve. Sure, it's good for people to watch TV together, but it's also good to know when to excuse yourself from TV and go do something more to your liking. Keep a book beside you, write a letter, make some phone calls, check your e-mail, do some work around the house, go visit a friend or neighbor. Come to think of it, you could try making these the priority activities, and use TV to fill in the times when they are not available.
- **Set limits**: it's better if you set your own limits. This goes for children as well as adults. A good idea is to keep a diary of TV watching for a week or two and then set aside some time to talk about your findings.
    - How many hours are you using up?
    - How many shows did you decide to see, and how many did you watch just because they were there?
    - What were the other things in your life that did not get your attention because you spent so much time on TV?

Then it's time to ask, "How much time is it reasonable to spend on TV watching?" Decide what is reasonable, then make up your individual or family schedules within those limits.

Parents can set goals for children's decision-making, and can help in making the decisions, but children are more likely to stick to commitments they have made themselves than to obey arbitrarily set rules. Remember, try to:
- discuss rather than dictate
- negotiate rather than demand
- restrict rather than ban

- **Beware of too much choice**: don't be foolish about your time allowance: if there's a long special that everyone wants to see, and that you all agree is important (The Oscars, The World Series, The Olympics, an excellent movie, etc.) allow yourself the occasional treat without guilt. On the other hand, be aware that with cable and video tape, broadcast satellite TV, and the increasing trend towards specialized, niche programming, someone out there is out to get your number. They try to hit your special treat button night after night with a 24-hour golf channel, all-day western movie channel, non-stop furniture renovation channel or some such. You can indulge yourself occasionally, but you're going to have to draw the line somewhere if your life is not going to develop into one long, non-stop indulgence.

- **Exercise the mind**: most of all, talk. Nothing exercises the mind better than a good session of talking. Talk to your partner, to your children - even to yourself - before, during and after the show. Talk back to the TV. (But please do not talk back to the cinema screen, or to the live theatre stage, at least, not until after the show is over.) Ask questions, explore issues, challenge assumptions. Become a skeptical (not a cynical) viewer by challenging and interrogating the programs you watch. Refuse to accept things at face value. Probe, look for the subtext. Above all, learn to ask the good old Roman question: "Cui bono? (Who benefits?)"

- **Challenge yourself**. Instead of watching only the same old familiar stuff, try a few exotic programs from new sources. There's no danger: if you don't like it, you have lots of other things you can do instead. On the other hand, you might just discover, as my sister-in-law has just done, that you adore grand opera, and never knew it before. It doesn't have to be grand opera. People have used TV programming to discover all kinds of talents and skills and joys they were not aware of, just by being a bit adventurous.

  Try it. Sample channels you've never watched. Use TV to broaden your mind, not just your rear-end.

- **Become media literate**: most people get most of their information through other means than through the kinds of reading and writing that are taught in schools. Few have any direct experience at all of current events, politics, sports, national issues, foreign events or economics. They do not go to meetings where politicians appear to explain themselves, nor travel to different parts of the country or to other countries to experience events and issues there. No, their experience in all these areas comes from the media, almost exclusively from TV. It is not an exaggeration to say that for many people politics, sports and news happen **only** on TV.

  Yet our education system has no program for teaching students how to "read" and "write" TV and other media. We acknowledge that TV is a very powerful influence in our lives, yet we do nothing formally to educate ourselves and our children to understand how it works and works on us. We seem almost to be putting ourselves deliberately in a position where the media can operate independently of our understandings of their operation.

- **Follow some of these maxims for quality TV viewing**
  - Make yourself media literate, and ask your local schools to include media literacy in the curriculum. ("If you want to use TV for teaching somebody something, you have first to teach somebody how to use television." Umberto Eco)
  - Know that quality is as much in the way you watch as in the program content. "A wise man will find wisdom in the worst of books, but a fool will be a fool with the best of books. Yea, even without book." (John Milton, *Aereopagitica*) Be wise.
  - Know also that any bad effects of TV are as much of the viewer's making as TV's. TV never made anybody do anything without their permission. Don't give your permission.
  - Consume TV with good sense. Set and follow a reasonable schedule for TV viewing. Avoid over indulgence or total abstinence.
  - Talk. Fight passive viewing habits by discussing, disputing and appreciating your TV.
  - Consume TV in carefully selected and fully considered wholes, rather than in fragments
  - Show respect for the good things TV can do for you, and for other people's taste in TV fare.
  - Be reasonable but firm about your children's viewing. Whenever you can,
    - restrict instead of banning
    - discuss instead of dictating
    - negotiate instead of demanding
- **Do something else instead of watching TV**
  - Exercise
  - Have a conversation
  - Read a book
  - Write to a friend or relative
  - Visit friends or relatives, or invite them to your place
  - Practice a hobby
  - Become involved in a community sport league
  - Learn a new language or skill at night school
  - Work for media education in your local schools

Ideas for Media Education

- Get involved in a community
  - Orchestra
  - Sports team
  - theater
  - choir
  - art gallery
- Make, build, repair, invent something

Watching how you watch TV can pay off in lots of ways; perhaps even in ways that this chapter has not touched on. It certainly can't do any harm, so why not give it a try?

TV AS SICKNESS: THE MEDICAL MODEL APPLIED TO SOCIAL/CULTURAL ISSUES.

I have a colleague in Waterloo, Ontario who regularly sends me email messages he has culled from the Web. Most of the pieces he sends me are about media, and are taken from newspaper webpages all over the continent. Here's the beginning of a recent one I got from him:

London Free Press
April 24, 1998

NOTHING'S ON TV -- FOR ONE DAY

By Hank Daniszewski -- Free Press Education Reporter

Students of Sir Issac Brock elementary school and their families will go
"cold turkey" on Monday. That means no TV -- for one whole day. And just to make sure they don't cheat, teachers doubling as TV cops will drop by pupils' homes, checking for warm sets.

You might think that I'd be delighted to see such a story. What better than to hear about some kids avoiding the ill effects of TV? Well, my short answer is, "Plenty." The longer answer, as you might have guessed, is below.

First of all, I haven't a lot of faith in instrumental answers to complicated, social and cultural issues. If TV is a problem in our society - and I'm not convinced it is so much a problem in itself as a symptom of other more complex problems - then it is not the kind of problem that can be treated the same way you treat a cold: with some instrument like a pill, or a dose of what granny used to call "cordial" or "physic".

Instrumental cures are effective in cases where there is an instrumental cause - a virus or a bacterium. However, where you get problems that do not have simple instrumental causes, simple instrumental fixes probably won't work. At most, they will work only partially. Oil spills are not cured by building bigger dykes around the areas fouled by them. They are only partially cured by better clean-up methods. To get at the real cause of oil spills, we would have to find treatments for human greed and stupidity.

The children in London were asked to give up TV for a day so that they might spend more time reading. Perhaps that is a laudable goal. Reading skills are certainly worth promoting, but it may be naïve to promote reading as being "better" than TV. The reason we want to promote reading is so that people can have access to information and culture. But most people now get their information and culture from TV. Shouldn't we, therefore, be interested in promoting TV skills at least as much as reading skills? And why do we promote reading *at the expense* of TV, as if TV were an enemy of information and culture? Why can't we promote both sets of abilities at once?

In the Nineteenth Century, when industry required a workforce that could read well enough to run new steam driven machinery, and handle systems like the post office and the railway, universal public education became the rule. But it extended only so far: up to about the age of ten or eleven. Education beyond a certain level was dangerous. People who could not only read but also think for themselves were not a desirable product for the industrialists and politicians who preferred a docile and malleable workforce. This form of controlled access to education gave new meaning to the expression: "A little knowledge is a dangerous thing."

Today's populace is in thrall, not to print so much as to modern media like TV, computers, advertising. Teaching this populace to handle modern media is crucial. For one thing, industry requires workers who can work with modern technology. Does industry want a populace, though, that can handle modern technology with critical insight? Perhaps it is now preferred for the populace to have skills and knowledge about modern technology so that they can operate it and consume it, without them reaching a level of critical awareness about the way technology works and influences society. "A little knowledge . . ."

SCREENING IMAGES

The London Free Press article goes on to give the name of an organization that promotes a "TV Free Week" in April of each year; a sort of TV Lent.

Perhaps Lent is an appropriate metaphor to use here as an alternative one to medicine. One of the ideas of Lent, as I recall, is to do without something you like so that you appreciate it all the more later. There is no intention in Lent, for instance, to suggest that meat is bad for you; more that you will appreciate meat more and perhaps more keenly if you do without it for a while now. This is different from trying to "cure" people of the meat sickness.

URBAN LEGENDS

A little while ago our family spent the weekend with friends in Sarnia, Ontario. Sarnia is a border town: one of those places renowned for cross-border shopping, one of the Canadian public's favorite ways of expressing its cultural priorities. During the drive there, our daughter was writing and rehearsing her speech for her school's annual public speaking contest (euphemistically referred to as "the oral communications festival"). Her topic was "urban legends", and she was enjoying telling her mother and me the sordid details of the fingers-in-the-trunk legend, and the hook-on-the-car-door legend. When we got to Sarnia, we talked about Jennifer's speech, and our hosts told us this story.

Some women who had been across the border to a mall were returning to the parking lot with their parcels when they noticed that some young, black men seemed to be trying to break into the car. Not wanting to risk a confrontation, the shoppers returned to the mall and called security. By the time they got back to the car, the men were gone, and there was no sign of damage or theft. The shoppers drove off to the border bridge. They hadn't driven more than a block or two, when the driver noticed that another car was following them. In that car were the same young, black men they had seen at the mall. The car followed them all the way to the customs barrier.

Not knowing what to do, the driver of the first car explained the situation to the customs officer, who pulled both cars over for inspection. Inside the hub caps of the first car the officers discovered packages of drugs. The men in the second car had apparently not been breaking into the first car, but hiding the drugs on it, so that they could later follow, find out where it would be parked and later retrieve the drugs with scarcely any personal risk in transporting them across the border.

Our hosts explained that one of their neighbors, a customs official, when asked about the story, had told them that customs had heard the same story, or versions of it from many different sources, and yet had no information to back it up. In short, it is a fiction: a legend. It is a story whose details are so seductively real and frightening that people want to believe it, and often refuse to believe that it is untrue, even when confronted with proof.

What are the characteristics of these stories? They often involve danger, or a very narrow escape, just like a movie or a TV program. They always happen to someone else, and are always told by a person who heard it from another reliable source. You never hear an urban legend from someone who knows about it first hand. The stories also often offer a chance to indulge in prejudicial thinking. The potential victims in this story are stereotypically female. Their devotion to shopping adds to the stereotype. The (alleged) criminals were male. They were young, and, most significantly, they were black. (If they had been unemployed we would have had a full-house of racism, ageism, sexism and classism. A complete set of bigotries, ready to be bronzed and.) The stories are often officially and publicly refuted, and yet stubbornly arise again, with few changes, often in the same community. People believe them. People base parts of their behavior and belief systems on lessons they take from them.

There has recently been a spate of urban legend stories about the HI virus being passed on by infected workers at pizza or hamburger outlets. This legend has refused to give ground to reason, and some restaurants have lost business because of the rumors. You've no doubt come across the legends that the Procter and Gamble symbol contains a deliberately-concealed Satanic symbol; that someone found a snake in the sleeve of a coat at the local store; that someone came across a deep fried mouse in a bucket of take-out chicken; (or an alcohol-cured mouse in a bottle of beer); that a man came downstairs to a surprise birthday party dressed only in his socks; that a couple changing drivers on a long trip, accidentally left their baby in its carrier on the roof of the car and drove hundreds of miles, luckily, without harming the baby; that a couple touring Mexico took pity on a starving Chihuahua, bought it and smuggled it into the USA, only to discover they had bought a diseased sewer rat.

Then there are the legends of the choking Doberman; the stolen child at Disney World; the wet dog (or any other animal) in the microwave; the corpse in the stolen car; the vanishing hitchhiker; the tidy burglar; the dead rock-star seen in the supermarket; the kindly Mafia neighbor; the pet crocodiles (alligators) in the sewers; the rat in the toilet, and so on.

Urban legends have been traced back to ancient civilizations. The legend called, "the mutilated boy", in which a young boy, usually of a different race or faith from the dominant one in the story-telling culture, is kidnapped and mutilated, sometimes ritually, has been traced back to early Christian times, and certainly exists in versions that are told against Nazi Germany, blacks in USA, and homosexuals. In 1914, when the German army invaded Belgium, one of the strongest stories in the British recruiting literature and popular press was about Prussian soldiers throwing babies into the air and catching them on their bayonets. This war atrocity legend reappears in one version or another, usually on both sides of the war, just about every time there is an armed conflict. One of the latest versions of it, of course, is the deliberate lie that the press swallowed about the Iraqi troops stealing incubators from Kuwaiti hospitals, and leaving the babies to die on the concrete floors.

Urban legends often take on the form of propaganda. Some of the seemingly harmless ones are told as a way of infecting people with irrational fears about others who are different on account of their race, age, gender, faith, way of life etc. Some publications - supermarket tabloids for instance - specialize in repeating and expanding the kind of thinking upon which urban legends thrive, and the kinds of story-telling that feed that kind of thinking: hence all the tabloid stories about aliens and flying saucers, legends that can perhaps be traced back as far as the Book of Revelation and beyond.

The media student needs to understand how urban legends originate, and to be alert for versions of them in popular media. The concept of getting our attention by focusing on our fears and prejudices is not restricted to urban legends. It is a mainstay of political propaganda, - where governments justify harsher jail sentences in times when violent crime is on the decrease – and of merchandising – where huge industries have arisen to sell us cleaning products based on our fear of being even slightly unclean.

Perhaps the biggest urban legend of all time was the cold war.

GHOSTLY LESSONS
IN MEDIA EDUCATION

The kids were watching a show called *Real Ghosts*, and I walked into the room to watch for a few minutes. It was one of those low-budget, re-enactment programs with cheap effects and no names in the cast. There was the traditional male voice-under, voice-over and voice-everywhere - the Voice of (masculine) authority - to make up for the lack of location sound.

I watched a segment or two. In one, a couple described how their life was disturbed by a ghost in their home. Actually, the Voice did most of the describing, with phrases added here and there from the family. The re-enacted events showed a young girl being dragged across the floor by nothing in particular, with juxtaposed shots of the frantic mother reading aloud from the Bible.

Another story told of a failed attempt to have a fraternity house ghost put in one of its appearances. The Voice told us the reason the attempt failed was, as someone later remembered, that there was a Bible in the room at the time. Another time, I heard the Voice equating ghosts with Satan, as if this was absolute and accepted common knowledge.

I was astonished. Usually, these low budget reconstruction are just fill: something to titillate the audience and keep them away from the zapper until after the next commercial. But this program had a twist. It wasn't just empty mindlessness, it was an active promotion of a particular kind of mindset, the kind required by some kinds and sects of fundamentalist religions, in this case Christian.

In a way, the program was the equivalent of Christian rock music: an example of the appropriation of a secular cultural form to a religious/political agenda. The viewer might have thought the program was about ghosts and fantasy, but the producers had no doubts about the fact that it was proselytizing on behalf of a set of beliefs about ghosts, their relationship to a literal Satan, and the sort of religious practices needed to protect yourself.

I repeat. I was astonished.

Ideas for Media Education

Don't get me wrong; I'm not about to launch in to a tirade demanding that the media be censored of religious messages. After all, religion-based claims that most programs reflect, and perhaps even promote other sets of values and beliefs can not in conscience be denied. Almost all mainstream TV programming is very secular in its values rather than religious; democratic in its assumptions rather than demagogic; rational in its argumentation rather than dogmatic.

As I stood in the room and watched *Real Ghosts*, I started to seek the media lesson here. What was it? The simple fact that a religious organization had started to use popular culture to advertise its message? But that's nothing new - not since chancel drama, morality plays and Christian rock music.

Perhaps the lesson was that the religious message was being embedded in one of the cheesiest forms of TV around. That's not new either.

It was my son who gave me the clue. When I said indignantly: "This isn't a show about ghosts, it's a religious broadcast!" his reply was brief and to the point: "That's nice. Don't watch."

I retired, wounded, from the room, and later tried to figure out what he meant. Here are a few of the possibilities:

- what you don't like or approve of you don't have to watch
- sometimes watching TV is not a critical exercise
- sometimes subtext is so obvious it does not need to be remarked on
- some people can see subtext, decide to ignore it, and enjoy the program anyway
- the time to talk about any of this is later, not during the show.

My own outburst had been intended to warn, to alert the audience to the subtext that threatened to suck them into compliance with a certain religious/philosophical/ political agenda. My son's retort was a reminder that I have argued frequently in the past that one can watch Sergei Eisentstein without fear of becoming a Bolshevik; see Leni Riefenstahl and not become a Nazi; read Ayn Rand without devolving into an Objectivist; look at violence and pornography without turning into a thug or a fiend.

When I talked to my son again, days later, he told me my warning was completely redundant. The structure and purpose of the program had been perfectly clear to him all along. No problem.

SCREENING IMAGES

Father swells with pride at the image of son who demonstrates the value of being a media-literate citizen. Father still worries, though, for those citizens who aren't.

WHY BOTHER WATCHING?

When you think about it, watching TV is a really dumb thing to do. It's dumb because there's really no need at all for us to do it. There are hardly any surprises in what we see there. There is hardly anything that we see on TV that we couldn't see or find out about from some other source. Very little of what we do find out is useful, or worthwhile, or reliable. We complain all the time that the quality of TV content is going down the tubes. (no pun intended.) We always say that TV takes up too much of our time. So why do we spend so many of our precious waking hours sitting in front of the darned thing?

The answer's not hard to find. We like it. It's easy, and entertaining. It makes few demands of us as audience. It constantly confirms for us that we are OK, and that if anything is wrong, then it's because of someone else, somewhere else. What's more, it tells us that whatever is wrong, we can solve it by buying something to stop it happening to us, here. TV confirms us to ourselves. It tells us we survived.

It shows us the people who are less fortunate than we are, but they are far away, and we can soothe any conscience we might have about their plight by sending money to a post office box. It helps us feel both superior and philanthropic right in our own living rooms. It gives us the excuse to disregard the needy in our own midst, whose quiet requests for spare change we can ignore as if they were on another channel. It tells us we succeeded.

It shows us the kinds of people we should aspire to become, with lots of detail about how these people are dressed, what kinds of products they use, what cars they drive, how they talk, where they go for entertainment, what values they have, and what things, beliefs or people they currently despise. It tells us we belong.

Most of all it shows us stories with a beginning, a middle and a happy ending. If the ending is not very happy, then it makes us smile

SCREENING IMAGES

at the end using one of its many sentimental tricks. It tells us not to worry.

TV is almost totally predictable. We can watch ten minutes of a show and predict almost exactly how it will end, and yet we continue to devote hundreds of the remaining hours of our short lives to watching these endings. I'm just as bad as anyone else. I'll watch the end of a ball game when my team is winning (or losing) by a huge margin. I'll watch a movie I've already seen three times before. I'll watch yet another episode in a series that never alters its formula one iota. I'll stay up late at night to catch my favorite series that's in syndication now for the fourth time since it was cancelled.

Most people will admit that TV is as I have described it, and that they like it that way, and intend to go on watching the stuff.

Pleasure has a lot to do with why we indulge ourselves so much in TV. We like things that are familiar and predictable, things that stroke rather than challenge our belief systems. They make us feel comfortable both with ourselves and with the world. But surely, pleasure can't be the whole story: there must be other needs that are being met, and other assumptions that are being fulfilled for us. I wonder what these are.

Some would claim that people watch TV out of lack of imagination. Couch potatoes, in their estimation, are people who lack the energy or the initiative to get off the sofa and do anything for themselves. Others laugh at these assumptions pointing out that watching TV is a harmless way of passing time, and that people are perfectly capable of judging when they've had enough.

Yet others talk about the style people have of watching TV. Some are passive viewers. They seem to be engrossed in the show. Their eyes are riveted on the screen. If you speak to them, they are unaware of you. They are "gone". Others are active viewers. They are constantly moving their eyes over the screen. They talk back to the program, to the characters, or comment out loud about the situations, giving frequent indications that they both realize what they are watching is a fiction, and that they realize that its representations are open to interpretation. These people are still "there". Unfortunately, some of these same people do not understand that the same kind of bantering give-and-take with the screen does not go down well in the cinema. Talking out loud at the show is an attack on other people's right to "quiet enjoyment", although that expression is becoming a bit of an oxymoron with modern sound systems.

Ideas for Media Education

There is the talk too about the direct link between TV viewing and behavior. This argument is often brought up in relation to violence on TV and its effect on the behavior of children who are exposed to it. The same argument is used about negative representations of women or of minorities. Advertisers believe their ads make viewers behave in certain ways, so why shouldn't the values in the programs have the same effect?

Whatever the case, watching TV is a fascinating thing to investigate, even though it may be a dumb thing to do.

MEDIA WITH
THE
SEAMS SHOWING

Apart from those who were there, baseball fans and media buffs remember the night of the 1990 San Francisco Bay area earthquake more vividly than most others. If you recall, the earthquake interrupted a World Series game between Oakland and San Francisco, and the TV coverage of the disaster as it took place was an experience to remember. It took me a day or two to realize the importance of what I was watching, in terms of the media effect, and by that time I had missed the chance to get some once-in-a-lifetime footage on videotape.

At first, and throughout most of that first evening, there was an excitement that came from the unfolding of an event before our eyes. I noticed:

- announcers so involved in the events that they were unable to detach themselves emotionally from the job of reporting, and were actually listening to the input on the ear piece to find out what was happening, instead of just using it to get instructions. (Were some of them actually emotionally involved in the story, as the radio reporter was in the famous Hindenburg disaster story?)
- announcers making mistakes: getting names wrong, doing a lead into the wrong segment. (They showed us how important it is for them to rehearse the news.)
- announcers apologizing to the viewers for showing images of fires and destruction, and explaining that just because these were the images on the screen, viewers should not conclude that there were fires everywhere. (Why don't announcers and networks make similar disclaimers every time they present

94

news stories and images that could create a wrong impression?)

- a search for the image that would be the single most memorable image of the disaster; the image that would later become the lead in and lead out of commercial breaks. (How many were presented? The collapsed section of the bridge? The conflagration in the harbor area? The sandwiched highway? Which one became the icon? What does this say about the way we consume news?)

- a tendency to try to summarise the whole event in an ongoing tally of the number of deaths - a reason to keep tuned to find out the final score, just like the aborted World Series game. (Which network had the highest share of viewers? Was it the one with the highest estimates of deaths? The one with the most frequent recounts? What was the highest estimate? How did that estimate compare with the final tally? How can we explain the difference?)

As the days rolled by, the reporting became more controlled. The news stories became more like the ones we are used to seeing every day. The announcers were "professionally" in touch with the stories. The segments flowed cleanly one after another without goof-ups. The earthquake and its story had been neatly packaged for us. All the untidiness had been eradicated.

For a few hours, though, television had explored its real potential - the ability to bring us instant images of events as they unfold, without the pre-packaging and preparation that so often turn our news coverage into someone else's version of what happened. Even though we could see all the seams, we felt more in touch with the events than we do in a normal news show.   (We have seen more recent examples of this phenomenon in the April, 1991 coverage of the confrontations between Natives and Canadian soldiers at Oka, Quebec, when unedited camera-roll footage of the stand off was often shown over and over again without voice-over interpretation on the CBC News Channel; in the Atlanta Olympics during the panic over the knapsack bomber; at the catastrophic deaths of Diana Spencer and J.F.K. JR., when networks had nothing to report but kept up the coverage, anyway)

SCREENING IMAGES

Compare all this coverage, for instance, with that of the Panama invasion or of the Gulf and Kosovo wars. The seams in those reports were all totally invisible. Those news events unfolded for us on our TV as if they were made-for-TV movies. The beginning, middle and end were carefully manipulated. The military briefings were like sports reports, complete with line-ups, scores, high-lights, statistics and replays. What we were allowed to see had been vetted very carefully before it got onto the air. Details that later turned out to be inaccurate (the incubators story from the Kuwait hospital) as likely as not had originally been deliberate lies. People buy and collect video tapes of the "Nintendo Wars", but no network is making available its raw coverage of the California earthquake of the fall of 1990.

STYROFOAM
AND
MEDIA LITERACY

I find I'm forever teasing my daughter about her teenage way of talking. You know the sort of thing I mean: talk that is full of words like "like", and "you know", and "sort of", and "like that", and "and stuff". You get the picture. Let me emphasize, though, that I am teasing, rather than criticizing. She knows that I love language in all its variety, and she is completely capable of coming back at me with a list of the mannerisms in my own talk. She more than gets her own back. I tell her it's nothing but linguistic filler, and she makes jokes about dentists.

Next scenario: I'm watching some popular TV program with my family. Let's say it's *Bay Watch*, or some soap opera, or one of my own favorites, *Star Trek,* and I begin to comment that these programs, week over week, or day over day, contain the same kind of repetitive stuff as teenage talk: place-holders, filler, meaningless bulk.

Bay Watch will take two or three minutes of plotless time to show what I have named "video sunset postcards". In these, two characters, usually clad in minimalist swimming gear, stare into each other's eyes, and neck on the beach as the sun does a dive into the briny behind them. There's usually some elevator music playing in the background, and the whole thing seems to be timed to last until the song is over, before the plot can click back into gear, and the scriptwriter back on the payroll.

Soap operas repeat the dialogue all the time. One character will get a line out, with great dramatic pausing and much looking at the floor (or ceiling), and, bless us all, the next character, after a long pause, begins the next speech with some sort of summary or paraphrase of the last speech. Then there's another long pause, and some more staring before the second character goes on to begin a reply. Then there's a pause, some staring, a précis, and a reply again. Seven or eight of these and the program time is filled right up. Most audiences realized long ago they don't need to listen with more than half an ear.

Star Trek, Voyager, uses the same computer animated intro shots for more than a minute of plotless air time in every episode. Think of the budget economies, week after week, when you need to shoot only 52 minutes of program instead of 55.

The ultimate application of this repetitive mode is the way some cable channels repeat the same four or six hours of programming in a continuous loop throughout the day. If you didn't catch the program at six, worry not, the same one is on again at ten, and then again at two.

You can't help thinking of the laundry detergent that is packed with 66% filler and 33% detergent. You sure get a big box, but - well, like - you know. Similarly, I am told, with ice cream: Some brands of "light" or - gulp - "lite" ice cream, achieve their low fat ratios by pumping more air into the product. Naturally, this "new and improved" ice cream costs just a little bit more at the checkout.

Next scenario: my daughter (same one as before) and I are unpacking a new purchase, scattering the Styrofoam chips all over the floor, and remarking how the box is much bigger than the size of the product seems to warrant. The rest of the space is taken up with the Styrofoam chips. My daughter, feeling a bit ripped-off, says: "This is the same as those TV programs you keep talking about, right, dad? All that stuff in TV is just Styrofoam. It's there to take up space, and pad out the rest."

My memory of how she said this is probably imperfect. There could well have been a couple of "likes" and "you knows" salted through the two sentences, but they were insignificant beside the insight of what she had just said. It's only when people use Styrofoam talk as a substitute for substance that it is annoying, and these two sentences of hers had enough substance to justify quite a bit of careful packaging.

She had taught me an important lesson in media education: all communication has its own Styrofoam - parts that are bulky but full of air. As Macbeth in the Scottish play puts it: "Full of wind and fury, yet signifying nothing". Often, these parts are nothing more than an annoyance, and the original would be better off without them completely. Occasionally, the Styrofoam serves a useful purpose, is not excessive, and really does enhance and cushion all around it.

An example that comes to mind is the bicycle sequence in *Butch Cassidy And The Sundance Kid*. This was one of the earliest popular music videos to be inserted into a feature film, but one which was there for better reasons than to spin out the length of the movie to a requisite number of minutes, to hide the inadequacy of the story, or to provide employment to some new starlet at the studio.

It used to be the fashion to suspend the action of many movies - usually when the central characters were in some night club or restaurant - to include a musical number. Some of the films needed only the very flimsiest of excuses to do this. Roy Rogers would give up fighting the bad guys long enough to serenade Trigger; Bing Crosby, Bob Hope and Dorothy Lamour would stop playing pat-a-cake to croon a witty ditty; even Laurel and Hardy, once they had learned to talk did the occasional soft shoe with lyrical accompaniment.

Padding.

In the great *Casablanca*, there are two or three musical numbers, but they are part and parcel of the drama, rather than just musical interludes. The best remembered of these - "play it, Sam, play it" - becomes a signifier of all that went on between Bogey and Bergman in those heady days in Paris. The Marseillaise number, when the German soldiers' bellowed marching song is drowned out by the singing and playing of the French national anthem by the other customers at Rick's Place, is strong enough to act as an archetype of the expression "dramatic significance".

In newspapers, it's not hard to spot the Styrofoam. Plenty stories are included simply to pad out the pages so that the ads are not too close together. In the *Toronto Sun*, and, presumably, in all major tabloids, there are lots of short articles that are included only to fill in the space between the ads. These fillers seem often to be indiscriminately slopped in off the news-wires to provide a couple of column inches at the top of the page. This makes subscribers who are looking for something to read pause long enough to give the ad below time to register.

Some newspapers, usually the local weekly variety, have given up all pretense of being actual carriers of eventful news, and have renamed themselves *Shoppers' News* (often without the apostrophe). It is doubtful if any of the employees at these newspapers are reporters. Nearly all of them are there to accept ads and press releases, to mail out bills, and to keep the books. It is quite interesting to take one of these papers and analyze the actual copy to see how much of it is related directly to something that is advertised somewhere else in the same issue. The answer sometimes is, "all of it."

We now use the expression "Styrofoam" in my family to describe anything in a popular culture text that we think is just filler, repetitious, or plain redundant. A litmus test for TV is to watch a program on videotape, and use the fast-forward control to surf through the Styrofoam. Having done that, it's interesting to reflect on what you wanted to get past, what you wanted to get to, and why.

Another test is to take one of those huge weekend editions of a daily newspaper, and do a quick sort of the sections you actually wish to spend a little time with. Then, reflect on why each section ended up in each pile. You can repeat the exercise with each page in each section, if you are interested in being more detailed.

My family has agreed, though, that not all Styrofoam is bad, and that sometimes, even when the Styrofoam is really obvious, it can be quite enjoyable. When the soap opera is a personal favorite, you relish the way it is extended for you by the filler. You contribute to the teasingly slow pace of the plot development, and you enjoy the suspense. You appreciate the fact that if you miss an episode or two, it's easy for you to catch up.

Occasionally, you look forward to the arrival of the *Shoppers' News* because you are eager to find an ad for a product you want to buy.

When you watch *Bay Watch* habitually, the visual side-trips are often as important as the story. And, let's face it, politically correct or not, those bodies are displayed there at such languorous length, because lots of people enjoy looking at them. Popularity is what gives popular culture its name.

When you are an utter fan of baseball, all the Styrofoam chatter that the radio commentators use to back-fill the dead-spots in the game takes on a relevance almost as important as the game itself.

The media lesson in all of this is one whose usefulness is in developing an awareness, and then in allowing yourself lots of leeway in exercising it. Heaven forbid that we should come to think of all Styrofoam as bad, or even that some kinds of Styrofoam are always bad. One of the most important functions of popular culture is to give pleasure, and we should be very careful indeed about getting judgmental about what is worthy of giving pleasure and what is not.

Ideas for Media Education

It is popular because people like it, not because it meets any set of rigorous critical or political standards.

If you know Styrofoam when you see it, then you are in a position to make up your own mind about its value. People who know how to make their own decisions are the backbone of a (media) literate, democratic society. People who swallow cultural texts whole and uncritically are asking for that particular kind of indigestion that demagogues of all kinds grow fat on.

THE CAMERA ALWAYS LIES

I spent a couple of hours recently going over old photographs with my daughter. We kept coming across pictures of her when she was younger, and she asked if we could throw some of the pictures away. Why did she want to do this? Simply because she didn't like the way the camera "made her look". Even at the age of ten, she knows that the pictures she was looking at were not so much a reflection of any reality that existed at the moment they were taken, as they were a representation of that moment, (or rather of part of it), a version of it, an interpretation of it - to her mind, a misinterpretation of it. She was clearly objecting to the interpretation, not the picture. Still, we didn't throw any away.

This incident helped me to recall a number of other examples where reality and the camera's version of it were widely separated.

My brother once gave me a pair of tickets to a Toronto Maple Leafs game. Since the price was right, and since my son likes hockey, the two of us went. It was a first experience for both of us. On the way home, we spent most of our time talking about how the real game to us was not as exciting as the TV game. We missed the replays, the close-ups, the commentary/interpretation. When left to interpret the game for ourselves, we were at a loss. We haven't been back.

This same son and I, whenever we go to a baseball game, are always sure to take along our headset radios, so that we can both watch the game "in the flesh" and have it versioned and interpreted for us by the radio commentators. We note, with interest, however, that the decision of the umpire takes precedence over the evidence of the media experts, and that the large screen, Skydome Jumbotron never replays any controversial decisions. Obviously, the judgement of the umpires is not to be compared with any evidence presented, slowed down, stop-framed and blown up by the stadium TV cameras.

Ideas for Media Education

In the early days of motion pictures, the producers quickly discovered that the klieg.. lights and the black and white film of the day were unflattering to their actors. Details of facial expression were hard to capture; ordinary make up didn't help. So they developed a kind of make up that was more clay-colored than skin-colored, and used it as a staple in the feature film industry for years.

Consider this scene: A group of about a dozen protesters parades in a street, holding placards in the air. A TV news team has been sent to cover the event, but there are not enough in the parade to make a good picture. The reporter sets up the camera and the paraders move in closer together, walking in a tighter formation. They all want to be on TV. The pictures on that night's newscast show close-up shots of what looks like a large group of protesters, jostling shoulder to shoulder.

Or this: A TV interviewer, the interview over, finishes off the shoot by having the camera operator take "cutaway" shots of her smiling in agreement, nodding, looking emotionally involved, repeating some of the questions from the interview, some of them, perhaps, slightly changed from the actual questions asked a few minutes earlier. Some of these pictures of the interviewer will later appear intercut with the actual interview footage, as the editor cuts away from the person interviewed to the reporter.

Or this: A news program on the topic of student revolt, uses an image of a burning flag behind its opening credits. The flag burning did not take place as part of the events to be reported in the program. The footage was taken out of the TV station library of stock shots. Still, these students are known forever as flag-burners.

Or this: A news team is sent to cover an emergency. The cameras never go anywhere without police protection. The only people who get to be interviewed are the police or other authorities. Some people are shown being arrested and taken away, but a request to interview them on camera is denied. That day's news report does not mention the attempted interview, or the refusal of permission.

We're a very sophisticated visual society. We understand that the Hollywood film-makers and their counterparts around the world have developed many ways of creating the impression of a thing happening without actually having to go to the expense of making it happen. We are quite content to see models of ships fighting momentous battles at sea; we accept that horses and space ships go faster when the camera is cranked slower than usual; we understand that prehistoric monsters are hard to find and that they are usually represented in films through the use of special effects; we go to films sometimes just to see the quality of the special effects. (Some might say that the recent release of *Titanic, Matrix* and *Star Wars, The Phantom Menace* seem to suggest that film-makers and –goers alike are beginning to mistake special effects for quality and substance in films.) We understand and make allowances for the artifice of the film-maker in fiction films and programs, and yet we demand of the news media that the materials they show to us on our daily TV broadcasts should compete with that fiction material. A news broadcast that consists only of studio shots, with no location film of important events, is not likely to capture many faithful viewers. The pressure is on the news programs to use all the visual techniques and gimmicks of the entertainment film industry, just to get our attention. There is now a growing tendency in news programs to show us a re-enactment of an event, when real footage is not available.

Much of this growing confusion about the boundaries between fiction and non-fiction comes from our own insatiable addiction to story. As an audience, we are so hooked on narrative that we can scarcely give attention to anything as abstract as an argument unless it is dressed up with a beginning, middle, and end, and fitted out with a suitable set of suspenses, a climax, and a satisfactorily happy ending. John Stoneman, one of the world's greatest underwater photographers, was virtually unknown until he produced the series, *The Last Frontier*. Each episode has an artificially imposed dramatic structure, which, as viewers who take the time to think about it will quickly realize, can only have been developed after the fact. Straight documentary scenes of underwater exploration don't always provide the excitement of discovery. The audience (and the sponsor) is far more appreciative when the discovered artefact is buried again in the silt and dramatically re-discovered for the benefit of the camera. There are now cable channels which specialize in adding narrative to historical and natural events, believing that audiences can not stomach them otherwise.

Some people will remember the famous sequence from Walt Disney's *The Living Desert* in which a pair of scorpions were shown dancing together to Latin rhythms. It was later revealed that the sequence was shot on a sand table, not in the desert, and that the gyrations of the dance were created by reversing the film, rather like a "Miss Mew" commercial. Still, the documentary offered the footage as educational evidence of the behavior of scorpions in the desert.

Ideas for Media Education

It hardly matters what the circumstances are: it doesn't take a person long to realize that there is no such thing as objective reporting; that no picture can possibly tell the whole truth, even if only because the camera does not have the range of vision of the human eye; that no report is free of some sort of interpretative bias; that any message we receive through any of the mass media is, almost by definition, only a version, a selection, an interpretation of reality, an attempt to make us see something the way the maker of the image wanted us to see it.

This realization is one of the most important understandings that a student of media will ever have: All media are engines that construct reality for their consumers.

The camera always lies, even when it is trying its hardest to tell us the truth.

Well, maybe things aren't all as bad as I make them out. Seeing the artifice in media can be enjoyable.

While watching *Planet of the Apes* for the umpteenth time one Sunday afternoon, I watched the Earthly astronauts plodding through a desert, in danger of running out of water soon, convinced that they are on a barren, uninhabit/ed/able planet. They trudge over yet another dune. But wait a minute, whose footprints are those in the sand ahead of them? Haven't they noticed them? What are they - blind or stupid? The answer is: "They are in take two." The footprints are from the first time they made the trip over the dune, when the camera ran out of film, or the sun got in the lens, or some other catastrophe made it necessary to shoot the scene again. Either time or budget made it impossible to erase the evidence of take one.

Some films and TV shows, particularly I suspect, those made in Canada masquerading as US, have scenes of characters in their shirt-sleeves at outdoor BBQ parties, with condensation showing on their breath and dialogue. You get the same thing with young lovers clad for summer, necking on the porch, producing steam all right, but from the cold not the heat.

Maybe you've also seen shows where idyllic outdoor scenes have been shot in the rain, not because the script called for it, so much as because the weather provided it. I remember one Christmas special years ago, in which a magic clown-like character was able to work all kinds of miracles, except the one that might have kept him dry.

Well, one of the dangers of knowing how to deconstruct pictures that you see, is that sometimes, you are going to find yourself laughing, or at least chuckling at a time when you are supposed to be experiencing some very different emotions. It's one of the dangers of being media literate. Sometimes your enjoyment is interrupted by some part of the program that leaps out at you and says: "I am part of the pretense."

So, breaking the illusion doesn't seem necessarily to break the enjoyment. Hordes of people used to flock to midnight screening of *The Rocky Horror Picture Show* to enjoy sending up all the obvious construction in that movie..

Those who remember the old Buck Rogers serials, or who have caught them on TV, will recall that Buck's spaceships regularly gave off exhaust smoke that seemed to travel faster than the ship itself, overtaking it in some scenes. And how likely is it that Buck would ever succeed in jumping off one spaceship and landing safely on another? But in those days, before Scotty beamed anyone anywhere, that was the way you jumped ship.

So where does all this lead us?

Maybe a couple of places.

First, it seems to me that audiences can know full well that their media are shadows – not real. We can be aware that it is all a subterfuge, and willingly subscribe, forgiving warts when we see them, for the enjoyment of it. The recent success of *Titanic* seems to confirm that we enjoy being cheated into seeing things that could not possibly have happened, probably for no deeper reason than that it gives us pleasure. Knowing that the film is a pretence has made it more, not less popular.

Second, it is important for media teachers to help students come to the point where they can discriminate between different situations with insight based on deconstruction. When should the insight be used to criticize or challenge the work, and when should it be ignored in the interest of pleasure?

Finally, it is important in media education not to undermine the pleasure that our students and we take from the media - vitally important, too, not to undervalue it.

SEASONAL LESSONS IN MEDIA EDUCATION

Christmas, as always, is just around the corner. Last year, I sat down in a very self-satisfied way with the TV guide, and highlighted (highlit?) all the old movies I promised myself I'd take the time to watch. Sheer enjoyment was what I was after.

This was the list: an absolute feast of Bing Crosby -

Going My Way
The Bells Of Saint Mary's
Holiday Inn
White Christmas

As an added treat, I was able to see all of them in their original black and white versions - except, of course, *White Christmas* - and without commercials. Imagine the anticipation!

And I did enjoy them all - very much. But at the end of the binge, there was a lesson in media education that I could not avoid.

I told my wife, who had watched the movies with me, how there was some disappointment built into the experience, too. (My children would normally have been subjected to this same revelation, except, as you recall, the films had been b/w and so the children had not watched: another lesson for another time.) Try as I could, I was not able to look at these films with a totally dispassionate eye. They all contained scenes or aspects that I had forgotten from past viewings, that now seemed to loom large in my reactions.

Take *Going My Way*, (1944) for instance. As it started, I had all kinds of warm feelings about an era of family movies, epitomized by Bing Crosby and softly sentimental, religious content; smooth, fuzzy stories and relationships; ready packaged values; bring-along-the-kiddies, no-thinking-required, sort of stuff. And so it was - for the most part - pretty well up to the end, or close to it.

Remember how the story goes? The landlord's son, Mitchell, has done the right thing and married the ingenue, compounding his heroic qualities by enlisting in the air force. Then there is the set piece production number of Crosby conducting the cherubic boys' choir and guest operatic soloist singing the title song. A nice touch, that: equating the young man's departure for battle with the endorsement of the priest singing, "Going My Way" together with a chorus of vulnerable children well worth fighting for. Subtle.

(Have you noticed how Crosby is shown playing the piano in all these films, without ever once allowing his face and his fingers to appear in the same shot? How did I miss this before?)

The whole situation at the end of *Going My Way* is not hard to see as an allegory of the US situation in the second world war as it was trying to rebuild its ravaged position in the Pacific. The church has burned down, and a fund-raising campaign is needed to make sure that the parish doesn't lose its spiritual center. Supporting the rebuilding of the church is just an allegorical way of pointing out the importance of buying war bonds to a population that was by this time, perhaps, a little tired of more direct appeals for their savings.

I was surprised at the film because it tried to slip some messages under the door - so to speak - while I was busy mindlessly consuming its story and characters.

Holiday Inn, (1942), and *White Christmas*, (1954), were an interesting pair of films to see together, because the second is a remake of the first, with Bing Crosby playing a different part in each movie. But a re-viewing revealed more than just the surface kind of similarities. These two films, in their time, were far more than the family entertainment they claimed to be.

In *Holiday Inn*, there is a sequence in which Crosby's performance at the modest rural night club turns into a full stage-production number, complete with synchronized back-screen projection of military scenes. It turns out to be a shameless recruiting number for the American armed forces.

Forgotten that scene, had you? Well, go straight on to *White Christmas*, and what do you find?

You find a production-number at the end of the film in which the veterans of a W.W.II regiment come from far and wide, wearing their old uniforms no less, to flock around their now-retired general, swearing their readiness to follow him again, where-ever he might lead them. And when was this film first in release? 1954? Could this have had anything to do with the Korean war?

So why is this a lesson in media education? Many people might say - may already have said - that the films I'm talking about were never intended to be propaganda, but that in their time they merely reflected the style of all films; and anyway, W.W.II and the Korean war had to be fought and won; and that I am being unpatriotic in calling them down; and propaganda isn't always bad, anyway.

I would agree with all of that - sometimes. Remember, I said already that I enjoyed seeing the films.

What I would want to point out, though, - apart from the terrible logic of the bundle of arguments two paragraphs up the page - is that propaganda very frequently is bad; that in the very least it assumes that the public is either incapable of or not to be trusted in thinking for itself. Frequently, in its most palatable forms, propaganda will put forward ideas and arguments that are very popular, to the point where nearly all those who see it will think of it as something that agrees with them. Significantly, though, not something they agree with.

For instance, there is currently a series of Public Service Announcements (PSAs) playing on TV, showing very vivid and moving re-enactments of fatal highway accidents. Each scenario involves drinking and driving. They are purely and simply propaganda in an anti drinking-and-driving campaign. They use the techniques of TV advertising to sell, not a product, but a set of ideas and attitudes. Because we believe, almost universally, that this particular set of ideas and attitudes is good, we tend not to think of the PSAs as propaganda.

But that is a mistake. They are propaganda, and we should be no less diligent in identifying them than we are in identifying propaganda that promotes sets of ideas and attitudes that we do not admire or want to accept. If a similarly striking set of PSAs were to appear promoting racism, would we not be quick to condemn them?

Do we consider the increasing tendency for characters in films and TV programs to be returning to the Bogart image of languorously curling cigarette smoke to be propaganda for the tobacco consumption industry? Or do these scenes merely show people doing the things people actually do?

Oh, what a tangled web ... !

My point is this: we need in our homes, families and schools to examine the materials we view and read and consume with a skepticism - but not cynicism - that is constantly asking questions like the one above. We should be prepared to accept that in many cases our skepticism is unfounded. We should be able to turn it off so that we can focus our attention on the enjoyment of something we have decided is harmless, even though it might be, strictly speaking, politically incorrect. But we should never be prepared to give up our right to be honestly skeptical, or to make up our own minds about when and how to apply that skepticism.

Media education, both in homes and in schools, can produce a populace capable of identifying propaganda whenever they meet it, and therefore a population that can decide whether the propaganda is valuable or misleading. It is my belief that the only ones who would argue against a population capable of making up its own mind are those who want to control the public's mind, and who fear a public with a mind of its own.

Christmas, as always, is just around the corner. Watch out for the commercials - some of them are real killers.

SIGNS, SYMBOLS
AND
ICONS

Semiotics, the study of signs and symbols, is not in itself an appropriate subject for study during the elementary or secondary school years. It would be a mistake to try to teach the theories of semiotics as part of what students are responsible for knowing before second or third year university. However, some kinds of semiotic awareness are very useful and can be developed in students of all ages, without coming within a country mile of teaching the theory. Theory is for teachers; exploration is for students.

The study of signs and symbols is something that I see as being useful and interesting in the study of media. Semiotics, therefore, the study of signs and symbols, is a tool for instigating useful learning, rather than a necessary body of knowledge for students to master. It is one of a variety of ways of organizing our approach to the media so we can increase our understanding of media themselves, and improve our own learning.

I was talking recently with a friend who was wearing a button on her shirt. On the white circular button, outlined in red, was a black drawing of an ordinary wire coat-hanger with a diagonal red line drawn right through it. I had spent half that morning complaining to my children about their untidy bedrooms, and my immediate reaction to the button was to say, "That's the way my kids feel about coathangers". To me the line through the coathanger had symbolized a prohibition of the use of coathangers for hanging up clothes. Only five out of ten. The button was intended to symbolize a prohibition of coathangers, alright, but not a prohibition of their use in children's clothes closets. It was, as you probably know, a pro-choice button in the abortion debate.

SCREENING IMAGES

What a perfect example this is of the operation of response theory. My reaction to the symbols on that button was controlled by my own experience and background. There's no point really saying that I got the button "wrong". There is no wrong and right. There is an intended meaning, and a perceived meaning, but where the two are different, there is no blame or fault to be assigned.

My daughter, when first confronted with a universal symbol for corrosive chemicals (a skeletal hand immersed in a container) asked what that container had to do with pirates. She had just recently seen a TV movie about the walking-of-plank, buckling-of-swash and so on. In this case, the inappropriate response to the symbol could actually lead to a difficulty, but the fault lies not in the beholder, so much as in a breakdown in the universality of the interpretation of a common image.

In some cultures the gesture that people use to summon other people is to wave the hand up and down, palm facing the person being summoned. In north American culture that gesture can mean "hello", "goodbye", or "go away", depending upon the context. The intended meaning, universally understood in another culture of "come here" is not a possible interpretation at all. But think of the difficulties that can result from the different interpretations of the same symbolic gesture.

The world around us is full of symbols and images that are supposed to have conventional interpretations. We use these conventions to find washrooms, to guide us when we are driving, to know when things are allowed or not allowed (parking, smoking, making photocopies.) We can tell from a person's dress or jewellery what religion they follow. We know that a certain sound in a theatre lobby is a sign for us to go to our seats. In short, we live in a world where there are thousands of symbolic representations of other things.

Our media are full of the same kinds of signs and symbols too. When you pick up a newspaper in a strange city, how do you navigate your way through it? Are there ways that the different sections are laid out that help you to know if this is the news, the editorial, the business or the sports section? If you are tempted to answer that the sections are clearly named in print on the front page of the first section – try looking at a foreign-language newspaper, and surprise yourself at how many signs, symbols and conventions you still recognize.

When you are channel hopping through a dozen different TV programs, what is it in the one that you eventually decide to watch that helped you to make that decision? Exactly what is it in the car that you hanker after that makes it so desirable for you? How is it that as viewers we all understand and agree that some events in a story actually took place, when we never actually saw them?

Nearly every interpretation that we make of what is going on in a screenplay is based upon the way that we interpret the signs and symbols that are included in the pictures. We know that a fade means a change in time or location; we realize that a long fade to black after a romantic scene is intended to suggest what has taken place between the romantic couple in the time between the last shot and the next one. If there is a shot of water included in the transition – a lake or an ocean shore for instance – we are quick to interpret a sexual encounter. We very easily identify the good guys and the bad guys in stories that we watch, and we do it almost unconsciously by interpreting their clothing, their body language, their dialect, the cars they drive, where they live, what they do with their leisure time. We recognize the kind of introductions that TV puts in front of each kind of program, and we know in advance whether we are going to be watching a news, documentary, sitcom, drama, soap or religion program, simply by attending to the images that precede the program itself. When programs break these conventions and make us believe that we are going to watch something other than what is actually delivered, they are taking a risk that we will feel cheated. When we hear a certain kind of music on a soundtrack, we react emotionally in standard ways with the intended excitement, romantic feeling, sorrow, sympathy etc., simply because these kinds of music have become conventionalized to the point where they are almost literally symbols for feelings.

And we shouldn't feel that all this is bad. Becoming more aware of the process of responding to media messages shouldn't lead us into condemning the media as being evil and wicked manipulators. True, some of the most sophisticated exploitation of signs and symbols is found in visual advertising. True, some of these ads are so "psychological" that their appeal is very hard to analyze. What is it, for instance, that is so intriguing about our favorite TV commercials? How many different signs and symbols are involved in presenting those images? How do we explain our reactions? What is it in our favorite rock videos that makes the experience of them so different from the experience of just listening to the music? What is it afterwards that is elicited in us from the video when we listen to the music? How was the video put together so that these responses would be likely to take place?

Have you ever watched a movie and become aware that you were taking part in an experience that was familiar because of the patterns of character appearance, relationships, or action? For example, have you ever felt a twinge of fear when a shadow appeared on the screen, menacing a character who cannot see the shadow until too late? What is your reaction when, in the middle of a horror film, a character stands at the bottom of a staircase, and then begins to ascend towards the camera? What do you expect to happen in a Western movie when two antagonists step out into the main street of town, facing each other? What other, conventionalized situations are you aware of in the films and TV that you watch, or in the stories that you read?

It is probably just as easy to establish these story patterns for students through an examination of fairy stories and fables and their common character types and situations. Perhaps modern fables and fairy stories will do an even better job.

I remember writing a piece many years ago where I made note of the similarities between the stories and the characters of *Star Wars*, and *The Adventures of Robin Hood*. Essentially the two films tell exactly the same story, and contain the same characters, who have the same relationships. Both are about fair princesses who represent a deposed king, and are championed by an outlaw band led by a handsome hero whose prowess with arms is unbeatable. I went on in the same article to point out how the *Star Wars* story had benefited from a few borrowings from Arthurian legend, adding a Merlin figure in Obiwan Kenobe. A combination of Robin Hood and King Arthur turned out to be such a winning formula of familiar and predictable characters and situations that the film and its sequels set a new standard in the industry. Indeed, the next remake of *Robin Hood* - with Kevin Kostner - maintained the Arthurian strain that *Star Wars* had introduced, and took it further by making the Sheriff of Nottingham into a black comedy figure with a crony for a mother who belonged either in *The Wizard of Oz*, or *The Rocky Horror Picture Show*. (See APPENDIX: **LE MORTE DE ROBIN HOOD AND HIS MERRIE ROCKETS OF THE ROUND TABLE**)

A local radio station recently ran a competition in which listeners were invited to phone in an opening paragraph for a romantic novel. The competition was very amusing, even though my own entry - by some oversight - did not win. What interests the student of media is that such a competition depends upon the fact that such things as opening paragraphs to genre novels are governed by a set of tightly controlled conventions, in exactly the same way as fairy stories and fables are controlled by conventions.

In visual media, all these conventions are affected also by the conventions of visual media: the camera, the lighting, the editing, the music etc. A great deal of what we find satisfying in visual media is the fulfilment of our predictions that conventions will indeed be played out according to the rules. We know that the hero will not be killed; we know that the romantic interests will work out in one of a very few predictable ways; we know that the pace at the beginning of the story is likely to be slower than at the end (except in films like the *Indiana Jones Trilogy,* which begin at a frantic pace and slow down later to do the introductions); we can feel when a story is wrapping itself up for an ending; we can tell in the first few minutes of a film whether it is the kind that we like or not. The things in the visual media that enable us to make these judgments are the semiotic signs and symbols within the text. We read these signs as easily as we read the alphabet, and just as unconsciously.

WORN OUT: FASHION AND CLOTHING IN POPULAR CULTURE

"Attention all students and staff. The weather forecast for tonight and tomorrow morning predicts very low temperatures and a snowstorm. As is customary at Someplace high school, in these weather conditions, the young ladies tomorrow morning will be allowed to wear pants or slacks, but not jeans on their way to school. Naturally, they will be expected to change into skirts once they arrive in the building."

That, or something like it, was a not uncommon announcement during the winter at the first high school where I taught in Ontario during the early 1960s. Nobody gave it a second thought. Of course, "young ladies" wore skirts in school. What else? And just as naturally, blue jeans were not appropriate attire either for young ladies or young gentlemen. No question.

Skip three or four decades and the issues don't seem to change much. A recent newspaper article described how the principal at a Roman Catholic school near Toronto had decided the young ladies at that school would not be allowed to wear Dr. Marten's boots with their school uniform: kilts or slacks. Unfortunately, in the 1990s, this decision was not seen as being quite natural. Young ladies and gentlemen of the 90s are not as prepared to be blindly obedient to the dictates of authority as were the students of the 60s. Perhaps they are better at seeing the difference between authority and authoritarianism. The issue got a lot of coverage in the press.

Whether it's blue jeans or Dr. Marten boots, it is really the same. Something that was at one time a form of apparel out of kilter with the mainstream has been co-opted into popular culture and even sometimes into high fashion. The blue jeans that were originally the stop-gap garment of cowboys in the wild west, passed first into

116

working-class American standard garb before becoming a badge of defiance: witness popular culture heroes such as Marlon Brando in *The Wild One*. Through the 50s and 60s blue jeans became the dungarees of choice for workers in middle class America, but then crept into popular culture when paperbacks such as *The Greening of America* extolled the virtues of bell-bottomed blue jeans as the answer to everything short of ingrown toe nails. What had once been working class and vulgar rapidly was adopted by high fashion. The designer-jean was born.

Gentlemen who care to check will find that dress pants and shirts can now be had much cheaper than blue jeans and denim shirts.

Dr. Marten boots, at one time, were the badge of punk and skin-head hoodlums in the British Isles. It was even said that the color of the laces worn by these young people told you who(m) they had stomped or killed with those same boots. Mainstream teenagers a few years later adopted the Dr. Marten footwear and, of course, diluted or eliminated its original significance by making it part of their culture. Check in chic 90s bistros, and you're likely to find people of fashion (and age) strutting their Doc Marten's for their haute-couture, groupie friends to observe.

There seems to be a cycle at work. New fashions are first adopted by those on the fringes of society who want to use their appearance as a badge of defiance against mainstream values. Before long, teens adopt these fashions as a way of showing their wish to be defiant, without actually taking the risk of being avant-garde. Older people then elevate the same trend into high fashion to illustrate how youthful they can be.

Take a look at the history of popular music - jazz, rock 'n roll, rap - and you will see the same process in operation.

The principal of the Roman Catholic school, then, was mistaken in attempting to ban the boots which had already shed their violent and anti-social symbolism. That same principal might well have had second thoughts by remembering for how many years parents and teachers alike have fought with youngsters to get them to wear what used to be called "sensible shoes".

The question of school uniforms is a perpetual thorn in everybody's side. Students who would die before being caught wearing anything but exactly the same clothing as the other people in their group, will go to the wall, march and demonstrate against the imposition of a school-wide uniform. At first, this might sound like a contradiction. But it's not. What the kids are telling the adults is that they are very clear in their knowledge that they are not all alike.

A single uniform in a school suggests that all the students belong to the same group. This is clearly absurd. All communities of students contain several groups. One of the best ways of identifying these groups is through their clothing. There is no need to dictate what that clothing should be; the students do that for us. (If you want another way of identifying the different groups in the school, ask them what kind of music they listen to.)

So, those schools that don't have an official school uniform really have several different school uniforms dictated by the students rather than by the school administrators. If students who belong to the prep or neat set were asked to conform to another convention of clothing, they would fight just as hard as those students who feel they ought not to be asked to give up their blue jeans or black tights in order to wear a plaid skirt or gray slacks.

Where school uniforms are the norm, it is often a case of control disguised as tradition. Where school uniforms are being promoted as a desirable innovation – as my own provincial government is presently (and quaintly) threatening to do to all schools – it is most often sold on the strength of tradition but instituted for the sake of control.

Our clothing is part of our identity. It doesn't matter if we are students or adults, we express ourselves and (re)present ourselves to others through the clothes that we buy and wear, and through the way we wear them. The bank manager who insists on wearing the blue suit, white collar and plain tie is no less of a clothing faddist than the avant-garde artist who refuses to be seen except in clothes from a second-hand store. Each one is expressing a set of values and beliefs through clothing. Each would also, probably, assert that they were impervious to the protestations of clothing manufacturers who advertise in the mass media.

Acquiring and wearing clothes in the past used to be a very simple process. Often clothes were handed down from generation to generation. It was never frowned upon, except in the very wealthiest and most fashionable circles, for people's clothes to have originated many decades previously. Sturdiness and wearability were the chief considerations, and clothes were frequently repaired over and over, cut down, re-made, re-used. The expression "worn out" had real meaning in the centuries up to the nineteenth, which was, coincidentally, the century which saw the spread of technology-based mass media, and of the advertising industry.

At the end of the twentieth century, though, "worn out" has got a whole new set of meanings. People now pay extra to purchase jeans which have had holes deliberately and scientifically - one might even suspect artistically - cut into them. Distressed, stone-washed, sand-washed, frayed and otherwise imperfect conditions are sought after. They advertise that the wearers have gobs of disposable income to spend on clothing but that they are contemptuous of newness or glossiness.

"Worn out" can also be used to refer to the modern practice of placing the manufacturers' labels and names not where they used to belong - on the inside of the clothing - but now all over the outside, up the sleeve, down the leg.., on the hip pocket, across the front. Wearing a certain brand name of clothing gives the wearer some sort of membership into a club of acceptability.

Individuals pay extra for shirts or trousers which have a certain label because anything else would not be cool. People don't think of wearing the labels on the outside as a form of unpaid advertising, marketing, or promotion for the manufacturer so much as a symbol of their own moxy. We have somehow shopped our way into a position where we have to impress each other by making it clear which stores we favor. Manufacturers and advertisers bestow acceptability and status upon consumers by the generous act of taking their money.

And there is no use complaining about this. You can't go up to a person wearing a T-shirt with Coca-Cola emblazoned across the front, back and sides of it and inquire how much they are being paid to become a walking billboard. The question is redundant. Wearing a Coca-Cola T-shirt is a symbol not of advertising but of membership of a group that is not Pepsi. The identification of groups by association with commercial products has become not only big business but big culture. The latest corporate-speak term to describe this phenomenon is "branding" or "badging".

New advances in technology often show up as fashion quirks. New dyes at times give rise to short-lived fashion fads such as fluorescent socks or hats. Mass production and mass marketing make it possible to purchase a garment that is identical to thousands of others and then, through the use of other mass-market tools such as fabric markers, to individualize it and make it unique.

SCREENING IMAGES

Most modern cities today have what is known as a fashion mall: a huge shopping environment in which buying goods is seen as a recreational - rather than a necessary - activity. Tens and scores and perhaps hundreds of stores under one roof will offer consumers endless variations upon a limited number of clothing themes; for these fashion malls contain little else but stores devoted to the selling of human attire, principally - I might get in trouble for saying this - for females.

It is scarcely possible in one of these malls to find a product which could, with sincerity, be defined as essential. Practically every item for sale is a product of one form or another of popular culture related to fashion, jewelry, popular brands of fast food, music, or some other form of conspicuous consumption.

Frequently, the products are directly connected to displays of similar products in other popular cultures such as television and movies. Popular television- and film-stars are seen wearing or adopting certain styles or kinds of clothing which miraculously appear on the shelves very soon after the release of the program Sports and entertainment celebrities are used to endorse clothing products, especially sports shoes. Consumers are led to believe that they can become like the person endorsing the goods, merely by adopting the goods themselves. . Cable TV companies promise we will soon be able to order the clothes being worn by our favorite TV characters by clicking with a computer mouse on the clothing item in the TV screen. What a triumph of converging technologies!

There is even a nasty form of bonded labor that takes place in some of these stores, in which the teenagers employed to sell clothes to each other are compelled to dress themselves in the store "line" of clothes, which they are expected to buy as a condition of employment.

There are still hotels and restaurants where gentlemen are required to wear a jacket and necktie before they are allowed to engage in the rituals of public feasting or dancing. But scoffing at jackets and ties is no different than scoffing at the open collar or the sweat shirt: it's merely a way of expressing that people have different values which they express in different ways, and would like to impose on others.

The ritualized demonstration of social groups through clothing is as old as Scottish tartan, and no amount of griping will rid the world of it.

Understanding how it works, though, is a better condition than ignorance.

IT'S THE AUDIENCE THAT COUNTS

One of the reasons that media people have such a hard time deciding what will delight us is that audiences are very fickle. One year we lap up westerns on TV with such an appetite that it seems certain more westerns the following year are bound to succeed. But they don't - they flop, and situation comedies take over for a few years until audiences get tired of them and go for science fiction or cop shows.

Well, that is a fairly simple explanation of audience theory, and probably one that is familiar to most readers. It's still valid, so far as it goes; but it needs to go farther than it does.

Why is it, for instance, that I can sometimes watch *The Simpsons* and enjoy it immensely, but at other times, I leave the room and pick up some other activity? What accounts for the fact that men at a stag party will sometimes watch the kind of videos that would embarrass them in the company of their families? Why do kids tell you, "You know I've always hated that show." when they have been devoted fans of that same show for months? Why can we sometimes turn off our critical awareness and enjoy a show that at other times might make us cringe?

I guess the answer to all these questions tells us that individuals are not *an* audience, but *several* audiences. What's more, we can sometimes choose which audience we want to be at any given time, and shut off the other audiences within us. We can be totally aware of all the criticisms leveled at TV soap operas, and still enjoy them from time to time. We can tune in to the World Wrestling Federation occasionally, without fear that it will rot our brains.

SCREENING IMAGES

Sometimes we will choose to watch a Doris Day movie instead of Masterpiece Theater!

A cyberfriend of mine recently complained about *NYPD Blue* because it occasionally includes a scene with some nudity and love making in it. His argument was that he did not want his cop shows to "turn him on" sexually. Someone else's read on these same scenes is to praise them for being realistic depictions of people loving each other. Some realistic loving to balance the realistic violence.

Other people watching the same show might remark that it is very graphic in its depiction of criminal activity and the consequences of violence. Come to think of it, many people might make this statement and mean entirely different things by it. Some would intend it as praise of the program, while others would clearly see the same statement as a condemnation.

But these differences among audiences are of the standard kind: the kind that considers each of us as a constant, singular audience. It's when we switch from one audience viewpoint to another that things really get interesting. Each of us takes up a "position" as audience, and interprets the show from that position. It's inevitable. We always position ourselves as audience for everything that we partake of. Sometimes we do it consciously, and sometimes not.

Take, for instance, our ability at some times to be amused and entertained by the *Indiana Jones* trilogy of films, while at other times the same films make us cringe with embarrassment at their openly racist approach to Arab people. Remember the scene in *Raiders of the Lost Ark* where Indiana Jones lackadaisically shoots the scimitar wielding Arab man in the market place? Cleverly done! Easy to submit to the broad humor of the scene if you have positioned yourself to be an uncritical audience. But position yourself as a racially aware audience, and you realize why some people complain that "it ain't funny."

(Finding out more about the scene might modify our interpretation. There is a story that Harrison Ford was ill on the day of this shoot, already exhausted by the time the scene was to be shot, and that the crew was about to lose the light. Rather than fight the big Arab with his whip, as the scene called for, Ford joked around and pretended to shoot him instead, and the scene became "a keeper". Our natural skepticism , though, leads us to ask if this is a true story ora press release designed to defuse criticism of he scene.)

Did you go to see *Titanic*? If so, what did you go expecting to see? Did you build yourself up for a great historical experience? Were you expecting a spectacular presentation of special effects? A fabulous romance? How did you position yourself towards the *text* of *Titanic*? Were your expectations fulfilled? Do you find yourself sometimes amazed that other people admired the very parts of the film that you considered the weakest? Did you heap contempt on the script and the romance, but find yourself with a lump in your throat at the end, anyway?

Have you ever had the experience where you talked to someone about a film or a program you have both seen and wondered afterwards if you were watching the same thing? For instance, if one person decides to take the position of *feminist* to *Star Trek, Voyager* while another takes the position of *scientist*, the discussion they could have about the character, Seven-of-Nine would be very interesting, to say the least. You might even compare the debate to the one that has been ongoing for decades among readers of *Playboy*: "I buy it for the articles."

Were you perhaps aware of an ambiguity of your self-positioning as audience when you first saw the films, *Philadelphia* or *The Crying Game*? Go figure.

Of course, many texts - movies, books, TV programs, music - try to manipulate their audiences into adopting specific audience positions. Political texts - propaganda - do the same thing. Sometimes, audiences accede in droves, without thought. Sometimes people who deliberately adopt an "oppositional" audience position are ridiculed or even arrested. Being a part of an identifiable audience can be a risky business.

All of this can go some way in explaining why the debates over violence, sex etc. in the media are usually oversimplified because they take a single, unitary view of the audience, and an instrumental view of media content. A slasher film becomes a different text - not a single text - to each audience member, depending on the positioning of each audience member: amused disbelief, detached passivity, fearful identification, slobbering perversion, etc. Our reaction to the slasher film is a function not so much of the text itself but of our own audience position.

To return to my cyberfiend who does not like *NYPD Blue* to turn him on at the end of an evening's viewing, we might inquire, not if he is correct in interpreting the show as a turn-on, but why he chooses to position himself as audience this way, and then complain about it.

VIOLENCE, SEX, DRUGS, AND -ISMS IN THE MEDIA

One of the hottest topics for those who think about media today is violence. Is there too much violence in the media? Is the violence too graphic? Is it too easy for youngsters to see programs containing violence? Do programs that show violence stress the consequences of violence enough? Is violence made glamorous as a way of marketing media products? Are people made violent by watching violent media? Should there be controls on media violence?

Many of the same questions can be asked about sex and sexual content in the media. Is there too much? Is it there only to attract viewers? Is it sensationalized? Is sex too often connected with violence? Does sex in the media influence viewers' sexual behavior? Does sexual content in the media have an effect on sexual violence and sexual crime? Should there be controls on sexual content in the media?

Likewise for illegal drugs. Should drugs and drug-use be portrayed in the media? Do the media tend to glamorize drug-use? Is drug-use too often connected with sex and violence in the media? Should there be controls?

On these issues - violence, sex, drug use - there is a general consensus that they should be called "sensitive", and treated with special attention. Tobacco and alcohol, legal industries that have succeeded in keeping their products front and center in the media even when direct advertising is forbidden are still not generally included in this group as "drugs".

But one other sensitive issue, or group of issues, does not enjoy the same sort of consensus: the issues of the depiction of gender, ethnicity, faith, class and sexual orientation. Our media are still full of images and messages that women find demeaning; they are often still racist, (if not toward African Americans, then towards Arab people, people from South Asia, or Native American); they still sometimes show prejudice towards religions such as Islam, Buddhism, Sikhism, Hinduism; they still tend not to respect ordinary people, poor people or working people as much as they respect wealthy or middle class people; and they are still frequently biased when it comes to accepting differences in sexual orientation. Our media and culture tend not to respect people of all ages equally. Generally speaking, the very young and the elderly get short shrift from the media, perhaps because they are seen as unimportant in terms of consumer profiles. In short, our media are often sexist, racist, classist, intolerant of religion, gay-bashing and ageist.

These, then, are the sensitive issues that media consumers can address as they educate themselves to become media literate:

- violence
- sex
- substance abuse and misuse (illegal drugs, alcohol, tobacco)
- bias against:
  - gender
  - race
  - faith
  - class
  - sexual orientation
  - age

Some people just say: "Avoid it all. Turn off the TV. Throw the magazines away. Don't allow the kids to listen to any of that stuff." It's an approach that relies totally on avoidance, but it works, if avoidance is what you are after. What avoidance does not do is provide any answers to the questions raised by the issues. It basically answers all questions by saying, "Go away!"

Others take a different approach to the problem of sensitive issues. They want someone else to look after it so that they do not have to worry or take action themselves. "Get the V Chip. Regulate the media producers. Legislate it out of existence," they say, relying on technology and government action to do the job for them. This is basically another way of saying, "Go away!"

SCREENING IMAGES

This will work, too, but it will work at the expense of our freedom of speech, and freedom of choice. What's more, it will do nothing to educate the populace away from the attitudes that popularized that kind of content in the first place. It may substitute one kind of media content for another, but there is no guarantee that it will substitute one set of audience attitudes for another.

Both avoidance and passing the buck will make the material that we are concerned about go away, if making it go away is all we want. But I suggest making it go away is the same as brushing the dirt under the carpet. It is not a way of addressing the real problem, a way of understanding what is going on, and it is not a solution to anything.

Puritanism and prohibition are not the answer.

To make the technological and regulation solution work, we'd all have to agree just what it was we wanted to go away - and that agreement will be well-nigh impossible to get. There is no way we can all agree on rules for any of these sensitive issues that would make us all happy. Some people would argue that any violence is too much. Others would want to consider violence in the context of the rest of the media presentation. Some people would want to ban all references to or representations of sexual practices of any kind, while others would prefer a more liberal set of rules. Some people would refuse to recognize racism, sexism ageism, classism, religious bias and gay-bashing as issues at all, believing that those attitudes are natural and desirable, and that the people asking to regulate all these -isms are the ones who have a problem.

No, consensus is not possible, so legislation is not an answer, and technology will not work. There will have to be another approach to sensitive issues in media, and finding it is bound to be painful and hard work.

The approach that I believe will work is the approach of self-education. Individuals, families and communities need to talk together to examine the sensitive issues themselves, understanding always that there will be disagreement, and individual differences. Then they need to learn to critically understand their own views and to respect the views of others.

For instance, for some, the issue of watching *The Simpsons* or *South Park* may be a non-starter. Those programs may be seen as totally off limits to everyone. Fair enough. But that does not make the shows automatically bad, or the people who like them automatically wrong. Others may embrace the shows as an enjoyable satire of modern north American life, enjoy the way they poke fun at some of our taboos. One finds them offensive, while the other finds them creative.

But let's hope that both families, before making their conclusions, have thought and talked their way through a similar process, where they tried out these shows to find out how they fitted with their values and preferences. And let's hope that this involved more than a cursory check to see if the programs triggered any biases or shibboleths, and included a serious consideration that the programs might be more - or less - than they first appear to be, and that someone whose views differ from our own might be able to enlarge our own field of vision. Maybe that won't happen. Maybe we'll stick with our first impression. That's fine, so long as we admit there is always a chance we might be mistaken.

Of course, this can only take place when people are prepared to talk about media, their experiences and impressions. It can only happen when people approach this talk with an open mind. Where people have their minds already firmly made up - where people approach talk about media with the attitude that they will educate others to their own point of view - there is less chance of any broadening of media literacy.

As a tool to help with this educational process, to help us all in looking at media material that is controversial and challenging, I have developed an assessment scale. It is rather like the scales or rubrics in my own book, *ASSESSING MEDIA WORK: Authentic Assessment in Media Education* (1996, Wright Communications) in that it consists of specific statements describing different aspects of the media work at different levels. But it is very different from those scales in one extremely important way.

The scales in *ASSESSING MEDIA WORK* are designed to help teachers pass judgment on students' work: their video presentations, radio tapes, posters, story boards etc. The scale for assessing sensitive issues in media is designed to help anybody - not just teachers - gather information about a piece of media to help them understand it better. The scale is not intended to be used to decide if individual pieces of media are good or bad, of high quality or low, but only to help specify whether the piece contains sensitive issues, and then to assess the *personal* interpretation of the way the piece handles those issues.

As we have seen in the example of *The Simpsons* and *South Park* above, different people will be certain to give different reactions to the same programs. The scale can not do anything about that, and is not intended to.

Here is how the scale is organized.

It is intended to be used to assess the way media texts address the sensitive issues of:

127

SCREENING IMAGES

- violence
- sex
- substance abuse and misuse (illegal drugs, alcohol, tobacco)
- bias against:
  - gender
  - race
  - faith
  - class
  - sexual orientation
  - age

A common approach used to identify sensitive issues is to publish numbers describing the frequency of certain kinds of content. (Eg. four scenes showing people smoking, three scenes with heavy kissing, two scenes with partial nudity etc.) My personal view is that arithmetic will not help us understand the differences between *Trainspotting* and *Reefer Madness*; statistics can not explain how we should compare *Matrix* with *Saving Private Ryan*; logarithmic calculations can not separate *Eyes Wide Shut* from *The Playboy Channel*

In an effort to provide something a little more sophisticated than tallying, I have developed a scale which tries to assess certain **qualities** in the treatment of sensitive issues.

These qualities are:

INTEGRITY: how important (or integral) to the text is the use of this example of a sensitive issue? In a war movie, for instance, use of guns, killing, destruction of property, depictions of death can be an important part of the message of the film. The famous scene in *Gone With the Wind* of the outdoor hospital for the wounded is both memorable and moving for many viewers. On the other hand, viewers are not unanimous in assessing the violence in films like *Thin Red Line* or in some Martial Arts films. To some people the violence appears integral, while to others it appears gratuitous.

RESTRAINT: how much attention is paid to the sensitive issue? In a TV police program, for instance, there may be graphic scenes depicting criminal violence against women. The question of restraint asks if the depictions are sufficient to make the point about violence against women, or if the producers might have taken the opportunity to include more scenes of violence than the subject called for, to the point of being excessive. People have different tolerance levels for what they would call excessive, and so they would be likely to give very different reactions to shows like *NYPD Blue.*

CHALLENGE: is the sensitive issue included in the media piece for a truly serious purpose which might challenge and expand the audience's perceptions, or is the piece taking advantage of the sensitive issue to conceal offensiveness behind pseudo-serious intent? In a news report about a bad traffic accident, for instance, the producer may include some graphic glimpses of injured or dead victims. The viewer has to decide if the purpose of this was to challenge viewers into taking more care at the wheel, or to risk offending some viewers while looking after ratings. The recent feature film, *Happiness* would be a good example to consider in terms of challenge. Once again it is a judgment call for the viewer.

CONSEQUENCES: does the production show not only the sensitive issue, but also their full consequences? Does violence lead to pain and disfigurement? Does drug abuse lead to sickness and personal problems? Or are consequences sometimes inappropriately turned to comic or sensational effect? This debate rages long and loud in the way people react to cartoons, or to live shows such as *Power Rangers* that are like cartoons. In a film like *Trainspotting*, where consequences are clearly shown, many people make generous allowances for the content in the story.

GLAMORIZING: does the media piece deliberately make sensitive issues look attractive? Is cigarette smoking, for instance, connected to sympathetic characters, and shown in situations connected with pleasure? Is violence or sex presented in a way that excites and stimulates the audience without any good purpose other than excitement or stimulation? Some people would argue that there are no good purposes at all, and others would ask what is wrong with excitement and stimulation. Action films in general often use special effects and enhanced sound to make their "action" scenes – which often are the most violent scenes – appear more "attractive".

BUNDLING: does the media piece connect sensitive issues to each other to enhance their effect? Sex, violence and sexist language and behavior; substance abuse, violence and racism? A re-viewing of some of the movies of bygone decades can sometimes reveal situations where Abbot and Costello make fun of stereotyped Arab people while inflicting violence on them that is played for comedy. The same can be found in more recent films like *Raiders of the Lost Ark*, and *Romancing the Stone*. In *Natural Born Killers* violence and sex are frequently offered bundled together. Some viewers consider this objectionable, while others see it as satire.

So these six aspects of sensitive issues are the ones that are assessed in the scale:

- ♣ INTEGRITY
- ♦ RESTRAINT
- ♥ CHALLENGE
- ♠ CONSEQUENCES
- ★ GLAMORIZING
- ⦿ BUNDLING

There are three points on the assessment scale:
The references and depictions to sensitive issues in the media piece display a sense of responsibility that is:

Level 3	Better than generally expected in my personal value system
Level 2	Consistent with my personal value system
Level 1	Not acceptable in my personal value system

The scale works by describing each aspect as it would appear at each of the levels. Using **INTEGRITY** as an example, the scale looks like this:

SCALE FOR ASSESSING SENSITIVE ISSUES IN MEDIA

♣ INTEGRITY	
References to sensitive issues in the text are:	
LEVEL 3	♣ integral and important to other parts of the text
LEVEL 2	♣ generally connected to other parts of the text
LEVEL 1 © 1999 Chris M. Worsnop	♣ gratuitous and/or unrelated to other parts of the text

The entire scale, with all six aspects described is on the next page. The symbols(♣, ♦, ♥, ♠, ★,⦿) are attached to help make the scale easier to read and use.

REFERENCES TO SENSITIVE ISSUES IN THE TEXT ARE:

LEVEL 3

Better Than Expected In My Personal Value System	♣ integral and important to other parts of the text
	♦ restrained to the amount made necessary by other parts of the text; understated or subtly presented; does not steal focus from or interfere with other parts of the text
	♥ thought-provoking, challenging and/or disturbing
	♠ clearly and realistically connected to consequences
	★ clearly not glamorized or exploited for sensational effect
© 1999 Chris M. Worsnop	◐ not connected, or connected but responsible and realistic in depicting these connections

LEVEL 2

Consistent With My Personal Value System	♣ generally related to other parts of the text
	♦ sufficiently in tune with the demands of other parts of the text; obvious and unsubtle; sometimes steals focus from or interferes with other parts of the text
	♥ pseudo-serious, exploitative, apologetic-yet-graphic
	♠ generally connected to consequences, which may be little emphasized or presented as relatively unimportant
	★ occasionally glamorized, or ambiguous or ambivalent in stance on glamorizing
© 1999 Chris M. Worsnop	◐ clearly linked to each other to increase interest and appeal, but stopping short of bias and sensationalism

LEVEL 1

Not Acceptable In My Personal Value System	♣ gratuitous and/or unrelated to other parts of the text
	♦ excessive to the requirements of the text; blatant, crude and flaunted; takes the focus from other parts of the text to become the center of attention
	♥ offensive
	♠ not connected to consequences, which may be ignored, distorted, falsified and/or manipulated for sensational or comic effect
	★ glamorized, unrealistically desirable or sensational
© 1999 Chris M. Worsnop	◐ blatantly bundled for sensational or prurient effect and/or to support/promote bias

SCREENING IMAGES

♣ INTEGRITY	
References to sensitive issues in the text are:	
LEVEL 3	♣ integral and important to other parts of the text
LEVEL 2	♣ generally related to other parts of the text
LEVEL 1 © 1999 Chris M. Worsnop	♣ gratuitous and/or unrelated to other parts of the text

♦ RESTRAINT	
References to sensitive issues in the text are:	
LEVEL 3	♦ restrained to the amount made necessary by other parts of the text; understated or subtly presented; does not steal focus from or interfere with other parts of the text
LEVEL 2	♦ sufficiently in tune with the demands of other parts of the text; obvious and unsubtle; sometimes steals focus from or interferes with other parts of the text
LEVEL 1 © 1999 Chris M. Worsnop	♦ excessive to the requirements of the text; blatant, crude and flaunted; taking the focus from other parts of the text to become the center of attention

♥ CHALLENGE	
References to sensitive issues in the text are:	
LEVEL 3	♥ thought-provoking, challenging and/or disturbing
LEVEL 2	♥ pseudo-serious, exploitative, apologetic-yet-graphic
LEVEL 1 © 1999 Chris M. Worsnop	♥ offensive

♠ CONSEQUENCES	
References to sensitive issues in the text are:	
LEVEL 3	♠ clearly and realistically connected to consequences
LEVEL 2	♠ generally connected to consequences, which may be little emphasized or presented as not important
LEVEL 1 © 1999 Chris M. Worsnop	♠ not connected to consequences, which may be ignored, distorted, falsified and/or manipulated for sensational or comic effect

★ GLAMORIZING	
References to sensitive issues in the text are:	
LEVEL 3	★ clearly not glamorized or exploited for sensational effect
LEVEL 2	★ occasionally glamorized, or ambiguous or ambivalent in stance on glamorizing
LEVEL 1 © 1999 Chris M. Worsnop	★ glamorized, unrealistically desirable or sensational
⦿ BUNDLING	
References to sensitive issues in the text are:	
LEVEL 3	⦿ not connected or connected but responsible and realistic in depicting these connections
LEVEL 2	⦿ clearly linked to each other to increase interest and appeal, but stopping short of bias and sensationalism
LEVEL 1 © 1999 Chris M. Worsnop	⦿ blatantly bundled for sensational or prurient effect and/or to support/promote bias

Applying the scale can be very problematic indeed. Here's why. A scale looks like a hierarchy, and hierarchies are used to separate the good from the not-so-good. The hierarchical use of this scale applies to our **individual** assessments.

That is to say, if you assess a piece of media a straight Level 3 across all the different aspects, somebody else might come along and assess the same piece at Level 1 all across the scale. Neither one of you could be justified in claiming that the scale supported their opinion and not the other. Each assessment is **only** a personal assessment. In each case, the scale has served as a clarifier for arriving at a judgment, but the judgment is made by the individual in the end, not by the scale.

The standards are in the individual, not in the scale. When two people disagree over an assessment after using the scale, there is no question of right and wrong; but, because of the scale, there is a basis for dispassionate, objective discussion and debate, in which the two parties clarify for each other on what basis they interpret the descriptions in the scale.

Without the language of the scale, they would lack a common focus for the discussion. Such discussions in the past have sometimes degenerated into name-calling, resulted in entrenched positions, and achieved little - if any – enlightenment.

SCREENING IMAGES

Those who have answered the phones at TV stations, or sat on school district or library committees handling objections to books will know what I mean.

The scale then, can not really sort out good media from bad, but it can help you decide which examples of media appear good and bad in your own personal frame of reference. It can provide a basis for discussion of different frames of reference, leading to an understanding of how audiences react differently to the same media texts, and how media texts set out to appeal to specific audiences.

This scale is not capable of changing the media to make them more suitable to your tastes and preferences. It is capable, though, coupled with talk, of helping you become more aware of your tastes and preferences *if you use it as a basis for intelligent and civil discussion with others*. The scale will tell you the limits of your tolerances, and how those limits are the same or not the same as the limits of other people or other groups. The scale will not tell you which set of tolerances is right and which wrong, **and it is not intended to be used as an instrument in telling others that their judgments of media texts are good or bad, right or wrong.**

Except in the context of the give and take of civil, amicable and reasonable debate, any use of the scale that attempts to use it to put down one interpretation of a text while holding up another as better, is a misuse of the scale. It is a misuse because it claims that the scale has its own values built in, or that it supports one set of personal values better than another.

The scale does not have its own values. The user of the scale brings values to the use of the scale, and uses the language of the scale to clarify an application of those values. Someone else bringing different values will arrive at a different assessment using the same scale. Assessments are not right or wrong, they are either well supported and reasoned out, or not.

Teachers and parents, students and children, producers and consumers of media texts can all find positive uses for the scale.

It is useful as a way of assessing all the texts that you, your family receive or "read" as well as all the texts you make or "write". It can be used as a basis for family or school discussion about media, or even, with consensus, as an arbiter of what is acceptable to family or community standards – which, of course, are not always the same..

In schools it can be used as a regular assessment instrument to apply to all classroom media, or in media studies, to all media in general. It can also be used to assess the media that students make for class, although it ought not to be used to arrive at a mark, since, as noted above, it is not a scale that contains its own values, and so it is not capable of assigning a value to anything else. What its use can do is clarify your personal interpretation of the intention and signification of media texts.

In congregations and community groups, the scale can provide a common focus for discussing media texts and the way they address sensitive issues. In these settings, too, it should serve to show the variety of individual interpretations, and could well serve as a tool for teaching tolerance and respect for the views and values of others.

If, in one of these settings, a group of people found that their assessments were unanimous in praising or condemning a media text, this is proof only that the people concerned brought to the application of the scale an identical set of values. It does not make their assessment any better than any other, even if the other is represented by fewer people.

SCREENING IMAGES

PART THREE

IDEAS FOR

MEDIA EDUCATION

ACTIVITIES

SCREENING IMAGES

IDEAS FOR MEDIA EDUCATION ACTIVITIES

In their original form as serialized columns, many of the chapters of this book concluded with a list of classroom activities related to the individual topic. In the compilation, however, believing readers would prefer the text of the chapters to flow uninterrupted, I have moved all the activities into this last section of the book.

My belief about what makes a good activity is one that I have developed over a number of years' work at writing them. Some books will offer nothing more than a few questions of varying complexity, leaving teachers and students to figure out how to address them in class activity. I have tried always to go further, and I believe I have frequently succeeded in satisfying all the criteria I personally set out for good activities:

- the activity should specify whether it is for individual, group or whole-class work
- the topic, problem or objective should be clearly stated
- the process to be followed should be outlined
- the activity should describe a clear expected outcome or product
- there should be some indication about how the outcome could authentically be assessed, revised and presented to a real audience

No teacher or class can use more than a few of the activities listed under each topic. School schedules never allow for more than a quick, often superficial study of a topic before it is time to move on. This fact, though, has not prevented me from offering a broad choice of rich activities from which teachers and students can make their best selections, and spend their precious time working on tasks that genuinely engage them.

ORTHODOXY IS THE ENEMY

1.1   Compile a list of the arguments you have heard from others in criticism of the kinds of media you enjoy. Make a list of your own criticisms of the kinds of media your critics might enjoy. Try to get one of these critics to sit with you and seriously assess the two lists to come to some conclusions about your individual definitions of words like "taste", and "discrimination".(Look at **VIOLENCE, SEX, DRUGS AND –ISMS**)

1.2   Interview some older people to find out what their parents and teachers used to criticise about their media tastes and preferences when they were students your age. Write a short story centring on this theme. (Look at **YOUTH CRITICISM 101**)

1.3   Do you ever find yourself criticising the media preferred by students who are younger than yourself? What kinds of comments do you make? What are you trying to prove with these comments? What do the younger students think of you? Make a long personal journal entry in which you reflect on the way individuals and groups of people try to put others down through their media.

1.4   Practice looking at media for its ideological bias. What different kinds of ideology do you find in: different newspapers, magazines, radio stations, TV channels, news and topical programs, entertainment programs? Make a non-judgmental chart of all the ideological information you have been able to find..

1.5   Play the role of a person with a strong ideological commitment such as gender, race, or class. Select some media products (eg. an evening's TV schedule) and asses and criticize it from the point of view of that ideology.

1.6   Develop some instruments for locating and assessing ideology in media products. (Eg. counts of males and females in leading roles, number of minorities in positions of power, checklists of expressions/ situations that indicate bias, philosophical assumptions that underlie characterization, action, or resolution.) Apply these instruments and those developed by your colleagues to the media you are familiar with and draw up a report of your findings.

1.7   Conduct an experiment in which you try to indoctrinate a group of people into a certain set of ideological beliefs using media. Keep detailed notes of your experiment and write it up at the end using headings such as: objectives, hypothesis, method, audience, procedure, findings, discussion.

1.8   Role play some debates in class in which students research the stances of individual orthodoxies and then go head-to-head over issues in the media. Keep the discussion focused on the media as much as possible.

1.9   Design an activity in which part of the class will study a topic through investigation and discovery, while another part studies the same topic from work sheets, definitions, exercises, tests etc. Decide how you will measure the learning in each group to be fair to the process that each has followed. Make a display in class of your findings. Write a summarizing article and submit it to an educational journal for publication.

1.10   Keep a learning journal describing your personal learning process during a certain unit of media education. Talk to yourself in the journal about the relative importance of findings things out for yourself and having someone handy to tell you the answers. Try to come to some conclusions about the value of each learning process to you.

SCREENING IMAGES

1.11   Save and bring to class multiple copies of last week's
        TV guide magazines. Form groups of four, and then
        form pairs within the groups. One pair is to work
        together to agree on a schedule for one evening's
        viewing, while the other pair observes the process
        followed by the first pair. The four students should
        discuss the activity in the light of the feedback from the
        second pair of students, and share their observations,
        conclusions and reflections with one other group.

1.12   In small groups, study a narrow band of media over a
        short time to investigate the thesis that the media
        dwells on the bizarre, sometimes ignoring very
        important news stories. List the bizarre stories that
        were highlighted, and keep track also of the major news
        stories that you think were short-changed.

1.13   Hold a class discussion in which each student is
        allowed to recommend that one media product should
        be banned. Keep a survey of the kinds of media that
        students object to and of the arguments given to justify
        or reject their banning. Sum up the activity in a report
        which analyzes the critical assumptions used by the
        class, and the ideological stances taken in their defence

ADVICE AND CAVEATS

2.1   What is a mass medium, and how do mass media differ from other media that are not "mass"?
- look in dictionaries and encyclopedias for definitions
- interview a number of people from a variety of backgrounds to find out what the popular opinion is about the definition
- do library or a Internet search using the words "mass media" as determiners
- design your own activity to solve the problem

(What you hope students will come up with, without you having to tell them, is a definition that describes a medium as a means of communication, and a mass medium as a means of communication available simultaneously to large audiences in different locations, and which does not change from one location to another, or from one audience to another. Thus a rock recording is a mass medium, since the copies of it bought all over the world are the same and do not change. On the other hand, a rock concert is not a mass medium, even though there may be a huge audience, since the rock concert is not available in any other location at the same time, and different performances of the same concert would not be identical.)

2.2   How far back in history can you trace mass media? Make an oral report to the class.

2.3   What is the connection between technology and mass media? Present an illustrated talk in class

SCREENING IMAGES

2.4   Which societies have the most sophisticated networks of mass media? Which have the least sophisticated? Work with a partner to prepare a short audio tape report.

2.5   How does the presence or absence of mass media affect a society? Imagine that you were able to introduce one mass medium to a society that had never before experienced mass media of any kind. Write a short story about the effects.

2.6   What new mass media are beginning to appear in our society, and what will the mass media of the future be like? In a group of three, prepare a bulletin-board display.

2.7   How does your understanding of the difference between mass media and other media help you to explain the difference between: theatre and film; personal letters and circulars; paintings and prints; published photographs and family snaps or Polaroids; tailored clothing and off-the-hook clothing; designer jewelry and manufactured jewelry. Create a display with annotated exhibits.

2.8   How do technologies like the computer, the photocopy machine and the fax machine interfere with the clarity of the distinctions between mass and non-mass media? Hold a class discussion.

2.9   Is the telephone a mass media technology? Hold a class debate on this topic.

2.10   Tape record people talking about a movie they have just seen. After one minute, after three, after five, after ten, after thirty. Analyze what people talk about at first and later. Present your findings and ideas in a chart form. (One of my favorite ways of doing this activity is to listen to my friends talking as they leave a cinema and go to the parking lot. What I frequently find is that they begin with talk like:

> "What was it she said when ...?"

Then progress to talk like:

> "I loved it when they ... "

Then go on to topics like:

> "Why do you think they ...?"

And eventually, by the time they reach the car

they are saying:

"Overall this was a ..... movie."

The process of this progression reflects a kind of universal human tendency to clarify, rehearse, comprehend and finally assess. Knowing about this process can save you from embarrassing experiences in the classroom when you've just screened a film and ask for opinions within twenty seconds of the final frame. Of course, people are not always ready to give opinions, until you have helped them through the clarification, rehearsal and comprehension parts of the process.)

2.11   One group in the class promises to give up TV and movies for a period of two weeks. Another group carries on as normal. Both groups keep diaries/journals recording both what they do/watch and how they feel about the experiment. Record any questions and issues that have arisen from the experience. After two weeks the two groups switch roles, carrying on with the diaries/ journals. At the end of a month they all review the list of questions and issues and add to them if possible. Then they organize themselves into groups of four - two members from each of the original groups in each small group. Each small group then refers to the list of questions and issues and works out its answers to as many as it can. The groups then report their findings to the class. Class members write up the class report on the experiment for publication in a local weekly paper.

2.12   Take a newspaper or magazine. You will need at least three copies of the same edition - two to cut up, and a third to keep as an original. Work with two others to produce a version of the newspaper or magazine that is completely free of advertising. Cut the ads away and re-compile the news content to form new pages. Present your new versions to a few friends to test their reactions. Use these test cases to help develop a questionnaire for other readers of your ad-free paper/magazine. Experiment using your ad-free paper/magazine and your questionnaire to find out how people react to the absence of ads. Write up your results as a report that can be made into part of a bulletin board display.

SCREENING IMAGES

2.13   Generate a list of all the things that people do while watching TV. (Eg. talking, knitting, reading, ironing, eating, homework, playing) Compare this list to another one you make of all the things people do at the same time as watching a movie in a theatre. (Eg. eating, talking) Take the first list and modify it to show the difference between the things people do when watching TV, when watching video movies on TV, when watching TV at different times of day, when watching TV alone or with others, when watching different kinds of network TV programs. Compile all the evidence you have found into a report about how people use TV and films differently.

2.14   Make a rock video. Watch lots of examples. Classify them into different types, technically (Eg. those that are essentially a recording of a performance; those that are made like a feature film, and require complicated editing and camera work), artistically, musically. Spend time in class defining all the questions about making a video to which you will need answers before you can begin. Make a schedule for finding the answers to these questions. Make the video. Show it to other classes. Obtain their feedback through a questionnaire you have designed yourselves. Analyze the questionnaire feedback and use it to guide you in making a second video.

TAKING A
SECOND LOOK

3.1   Talk in groups about your own practices of giving only fleeting or partial attention to messages or tasks. Keep asking the questions, "Is this good? " and "Is this always good?"

3.2   Write a personal journal-type piece about times when you have felt that you were insulted by media messages, and times when you have felt flattered. (Excluded-included, patronized-challenged)

3.3   Try flipping through a variety of different magazines to identify the tricks they have to make you pause an extra fraction of a second on certain pages. Get together with other students to produce a pamphlet or demonstration describing all the various tricks you have discovered.

3.4   Working in small groups, swap stories about times when you didn't take a second look, and later wished that you had; and about times when you took a good second look and were glad you did.

3.5   Seek out and bring to class a number of "trompe l'oeiul" illustrations. The best known one is the black and white image which could be either a vase or the silhouettes of two faces looking at each other. Make a collection of such images, and add some of your own. Experiment with the pictures by surveying other students to see what differences there are in the way they see them. Write up your survey findings.

3.6   Look through magazines for full page color ads with hardly any print in them. Paste them on cardboard and use them in an experiment where you ask people to look at each one briefly and respond with a very short description of their reaction. Look for trends in the responses and find connections between the trends and the images.

3.7 Use the same collection of magazines in a study of magazine genre and audience focus. Simply take a magazine into a group and talk about its characteristics until you have developed a profile. Using more than one issue of the same magazine makes this activity more valid.

3.8 Use the same collection of ads in small groups to talk about some questions that might be asked? (Eg. why are these colors used? Why were these people selected? Why are the details of the picture arranged in this way?) A good way to find out which questions are important is to try to make a tableau out of the ad and to keep track of the problems and comments of the group members as they work on the tableau.

3.9 Arrange a day in class where each student brings in a favorite cultural object. (Eg. an album, a poster, a toy, a comic) Work in groups of three or four to examine these objects by taking two, three and more looks at them. Make group reports back to the class, and then arrange to make a video report on the four or five best examples.

3.10 Make a sketch, write a poem, design an ad, story-board a video that you hope people will give a second look. Write an accompanying comment on what you hope people will get from taking a second look at your work.

3.11 Interview some adults about how they react to the concept of taking a second look. Collect some audio tape of their reactions, anecdotes and opinions. Edit the tape into a radio documentary.

3.12 Make a point of changing one of your typical media rituals. Spend extra time reading the paper, or look at yesterday's paper again; watch that video again and ask some questions as you do; change the way you normally look through a magazine, or spend time looking through a magazine with a friend, commenting on what you find

3.13   Look into some seemingly "good news" stories in
        newspapers, magazines or video, and use the technique
        of problematizing to seek out the deeper issues that are
        unstated. (Why is the Caribbean vacation so cheap? What
        are the problems that underlie the cheerful story about
        food-bank volunteers? What is the basic appeal of
        programs like *American Gladiators* and *WWF*?) Test out
        members of your class to see how they react when you
        problematize one of their favorite shows. (*Baywatch,
        Family of Five, Dawson's Creek, The Simpsons, Larry King,
        Live*)

NEGOTIATING MEANING

4.1   Work in small groups. Listen to a radio in class, tuning it
       to various stations in sequence, taking your cue from
       each other as to when and why they would like to
       change the station, and which stations you like to spend
       time listening to. Make notes about your feelings and
       thoughts about each station change. Conduct the
       experiment on both the AM and FM frequencies.
       Compare notes on your reactions to the various stations,
       and focus discussion on your awareness of how you
       reject or accept individual radio media messages after
       just a few seconds' exposure. You could repeat the
       exercise, using the TV remote control instead of a radio.
       Ask each group to give a short report on how decisions
       get made by individuals concerning acceptance or
       rejection of media messages.

4.2   Ask two students who disagreed about a particular
       radio station or TV channel in the last activity to hold a
       discussion in front of the class in which they try to
       explain their personal points of view, and persuade the
       other to alter their decision. (Absolutely no "put-downs"
       or "dissing" allowed!) Discuss or reflect upon the
       process of negotiation between the two individuals.
       Next, complete a journal entry about a time when your
       reaction to a media text shifted. Share your journal
       entries in pairs. Combine pairs and discuss the process
       of negotiation that has taken place in the individual
       journal entries, keeping note of any commonalities.

Finally, pool the observations of the groups of four and try to come up with a working definition of the processes used by individuals as they Negotiate with a media text.

4.3 Account for the popularity of some TV shows which you personally do not like or enjoy. Watch at least two episodes or versions of one of the shows in question, and be prepared also to report to your home group or class about your initial feelings and opinions, as well as your honest observations of being forced to watch it. Particularly, be honest about reporting any changes in your perception or opinion of the show, and thorough in analyzing or explaining how those changes came about. (Eg. People who never watch soap operas may find some interest or fascination in them after a time. People who do not like documentaries may find some reward in them after all. People who claim they hate sitcoms, might find some that they actually enjoy.)

4.4 List difficulties you have had with demanding or difficult media texts. If possible, bring samples to class to share with others. (Some music groups may be more challenging than others; some magazines demand more of the reader than others; some newspapers are more difficult than others.) Try to focus a class discussion on the rewards that can follow from an encounter with a difficult text. Try interviewing the author in-role as one way of finding the rewards in a difficult text.

4.5 Take a look at advertising messages. To what extent are they designed to appeal to our habit of accepting messages uncritically? Which advertising messages do you tend to reject without much thought? Are there any ads that are deliberately designed to engage you in a kind of negotiation of meaning? Make a class display of the various kinds of ads. Attach notes to your samples describing how the class perceives them.

4.6 Keep a journal for a few days in which you keep track of your experiences negotiating with media texts.

4.7 Make up a survey to test students and adults on their attitudes to rock videos. Report back to the class on the results of the surveys.

SCREENING IMAGES

4.8   Prepare an illustrated talk for the class on the topic of how rock videos influence the style of mainstream programs. Conduct a class discussion on the general topic of TV style, and try to agree on some definitions.

4.9   Interview some adults of varying ages to find out what it was in their youth that their own parents objected to. (Eg. comic books, horror films, blue jeans.) How can these interviews help bring a perspective to a discussion of rock videos?

OUR MEDIA DEFINE US

5.1   Brainstorm with some classmates to compile a list of experiences in which you recall having behaved unconsciously or consciously according to some media model or stereotype. Compile an anthology of written accounts of these experiences.

5.2   Take a survey of class members to find which media stereotypes of behavior they find:

- amusing
- annoying
- dangerous
- constructive

5.3   Make some suggestions for taking advantage of the power of the media to dictate stereotypes or models of behavior in order to consciously use the media to **improve** the social behavior of citizens.

5.4   Read the novel, *A Clockwork Orange*, by Anthony Burgess, in which the topic of deliberate engineering of human behavior is explored. Hold some class discussions on the issue of behavior manipulation, both conscious and unconscious. Try to arrive at a statement of ethics on the topic by which media producers might be guided.

5.5   Consider some of the following situations and write editorially or in fiction using them as themes:

- an individual sees a crime being committed and is uncertain how to behave
- a person who strongly resembles a central character in a popular TV series experiences some interesting problems because of the resemblance
- a major advertiser finds a way to capitalize on the

way media consumers tend to imitate the behavior of media stereotypes

- a community group objects to a media stereotype they want to see banned because of its perceived possible influence on human behavior
- a family disagrees about what is good media and what is not

5.6   Make a class list of some occasions in life when sizzle is passed off as steak to an uncritical consuming audience.

5.7   Debate the topic: The power of the media to influence human behavior is too great to leave its control in the hands of commercial interests.

5.8   Explore the possibility that aspects of teen behavior (sexual behavior, violence, drug use, crime, caring for third world countries, caring for the environment) can be traced to models in media. (music groups, TV characters and shows, advertising campaigns, public personalities)

5.9   Write an editorial, a historical short story, or a science fiction story to illustrate the thesis: "Every age has argued that the sky is falling because people are unduly influenced by popular but corrupt models from dominant media."

5.10 Select a media stereotype which you feel may have an influence on people's behavior, and design and conduct a survey to determine how close that connection is. Write up your procedures and findings in a report.

5.11 Research some occasions when human behavior may have been very significantly influenced by media:

- Germany in the time of Goebbels' propaganda machine
- The western world during the time of the "Hollywood Ten"
- Soviet Russia during the 1920's when cinema was recognized as a very significant influence on the behavior and values of the populace
- Ancient Rome, when emperors offered "bread and circuses"

5.12 Work with a friend to make a scrap book about your partner's media tastes and preferences. Explain and illustrate the preferences in detail.

5.13   Set up a situation where you can interview some
        students who are years younger than yourself. Talk to
        them about the kinds of media they prefer, so that you
        can develop some sort of a media profile of them. Make
        a tape recording of the interviews, and listen to the tape
        again in class. Analyze your own reactions to some of
        the preferences stated by the young people, and to some
        of the explanations given.
        • what did the students say that you had expected?-
        • what did they say that surprised you?
        • what were your own reactions to their statements as
          an older person? (Did you want to argue, agree, put
          down, interrupt, correct?)
        • how did the way you conducted the interview define
          the relationship between you and the youngsters?
        • if you had to do the exercise again, what would you
          repeat, and what would you change?

5.14   Repeat the exercise above with people older than
        yourself.

5.15   Write a personal journal entry about the media habits you
        developed as a youngster that are still part of you. Reflect
        in your journal about the significance of what you
        discover. Share your entry with a few other students. Try
        to draw some general conclusions.

5.16   Select characters from fiction, (stories, TV, film, plays)
        and define them in terms of their media preferences. (Eg.
        what might be Macbeth's favorite film?) Make modern
        wardrobes and media profiles for historical figures. Add
        a note to explain each choice that you have made.

5.17   Role play a meeting between a parent and a teenager in
        which the teenager asks permission to attend a rock
        concert in another city. Bring out in the role play the
        conflicts or misunderstandings that might exist between
        the two about the significance of the teenager's taste in
        music. Develop several different versions of the meeting,
        with different resolutions, and discuss in class how
        meetings can stay on track or go off track.

SCREENING IMAGES

5.18   Think of a time when someone has recommended some
        different kind of media text to you. Perhaps they wanted
        you to read a book they enjoyed, or to see a movie they
        liked, or listen to their favorite group. What has been
        your reaction to such recommendations? How frequently
        have you been prepared to try out the recommendation?
        What criteria do you use to decide if you will give it a try
        or not? How open are you to new experiences which may
        challenge your way of seeing the world?

5.19   Take a new look at some of the media that you have
        made in your class as part of other projects. (Films, video
        tapes, audio tapes, magazines, newspapers, comic books)
        What can you find in these media that informs the
        audience about you, the media makers?

5.20   First select one person and ask what newspaper s/he
        most frequently reads. Give them a copy of that
        newspaper with the instructions to select one section only
        to take as reading material to the dentist's office, or on a
        long bus ride. Ask for an explanation of why s/he chose
        that particular section. Let the class discuss the
        explanation in the light of their own expectations.

5.21   Form groups no larger than four. (Each group is to
        nominate a process observer whose job it will be to keep
        notes and report on how well the group operates.) The
        task of each group is:

        •   to write predictions about how each member of the
            group would have made a selection of a newspaper
            section under the same circumstances as the first
            student. (See 5.20 above)
        •   to write down how they personally would have made
            the same selection.

        Each group makes a brief report to the class on their
        findings. Have one or two students keep a record of all
        the different parts of the paper that were selected and the
        reasons people gave for selecting them. Develop a chart
        to show the frequency that each section of the paper is
        read by members of the class. Is there a section that no-
        one reads? Is there a section that everyone reads?

5.22   Brainstorm a list of deletions or additions that you could suggest to make a newspaper more appealing to your own class.

5.23   Predict the changes of next decade for the newspapers you know

5.24   Have class members conduct some of the above activities in another class and use the results to compare with the findings of your own class. Revise your own work as a result of the new input.

5.25   Create an activity related to the topic of media-influenced human behavior, and, after confirming it with your teacher, follow that activity through to a conclusion.

URBAN LEGENDS

6.1 Conduct some sessions in small groups where you exchange stories that are almost certainly urban legends. Analyze each one to see how it fits the characteristics of other urban legends. Be particularly careful to identify any bias in your stories.

6.2 Search through your local press for stories that seem to be more legendary than truthful. Check back with the newspaper or magazine to find out how the story was reported, how it was corroborated, and how it managed to get into print.

6.3 Do a literature/Internet search under the subject-heading of "urban legend". Collect as many articles as you can, assign them to individual students to summarize, and hold a class reporting session.

6.4 Locate and read one or more of the books on urban legends by Jan Harold Brunvand. Report in detail to the class.

6.5 Research a single urban legend in detail, and make a full oral report on it at a school assembly.

6.6 Hold a class debate on the topic : "Urban legends are just good fun. They do no harm."

6.7 Write an essay about "tabloid thinking".

6.8 Use a video camera or audio recorder to do some on-the-street interviews on people's attitudes and beliefs about urban legends. Cut your material together into a point-of-view documentary.

6.9   Hold a group discussion to decide whether you think
        the mass media are responsible for the survival of urban
        legends, or whether you would attribute their long life
        to some other causes.

WHY BOTHER

WATCHING?

7.1   Pick a show that you watch regularly, and classify it as a particular kind of TV show. (Sitcom, police drama, etc) Now list all the things that you can take for granted about this kind of show. (Eg. Sitcoms often take place mostly in a single, indoor setting. Star characters in a police drama never get killed unless they are leaving the show.) Combine your lists with those made by other students until you are satisfied you have a comprehensive description of the type of show, or "genre".

7.2   Next, list all the things that you can take for granted in this particular show. (Party of Five, Star Trek, etc) Combine lists with others in the same way as before.

7.3   Last, write a statement explaining what you are trying to achieve or discover by watching this particular episode of this particular program in this particular genre. (To find out if two characters eventually get together; to see how the old formula can be given yet another twist; to enjoy the comfort of familiarity; to buy into the values of the show even more deeply than before; to confirm that your values, tastes, beliefs are sound.)

7.4   Apply the same criteria (what's predictable, what are you trying to find out by watching) to shows other than dramas. (Game shows, news broadcasts, re-enacted crime shows)

7.5   Form small discussion groups and talk about your least favorite kinds of TV shows. (documentaries, foreign films, "difficult" movies) and explain precisely why you don't like them. Cop-out descriptions, such as boring, or dull, are not acceptable. Compare notes with other groups and work together to draw up a chart of likes and dislikes classified by audience groups. Conclude with a summary statement about the role played by familiarity in the selection of TV programming.

7.6   Work with two others to brainstorm an entirely new kind of TV show that would have fewer predicable parts and more surprises. Test market it among your friends.

7.7   Investigate the topic of audience research as it is practised by TV programmers. What kinds of questions do they ask, and what kinds of answers are they looking for?

7.8   Schedule a week of shows that you would like to watch. Compare your schedule with that of another student, and combine them into a single schedule that has the maximum appeal to both of you. Combine with another pair of students, and make a single schedule again out of two. Conclude by talking about how difficult it is for programmers to keep broad audiences happy.

7.9   Debate the topic: "The only important job television does is to deliver audiences to advertisers."

7.10   Explore the connection between pleasure and TV by conducting a survey in another class. Work in a group of four to develop the survey after talking in detail about the kinds of information you would like to obtain. Summarize your findings for a report to the class involved, as well as to your own class.

7.11   Research the topic of TV addiction. What are the symptoms? The causes? The remedies? Create a pamphlet on the disorder, similar to the ones available in doctors' offices. Print your pamphlet, and try to get permission to have it on display in local electronics stores and other places.

MEDIA WITH
THE
SEAMS SHOWING

8.1   Obtain and listen to a recording of Orson Welles' famous
        radio play of *The War of the Worlds*. Obtain also some of
        the contemporary descriptions of the impact of that
        broadcast. They will be available in newspaper and
        magazine archives. Look for websites on the topic. Ask
        your librarian to help you find some of the articles written
        by sociologists and communications theorists about this
        same broadcast. (You could substitute reports of the
        Hindenburg disaster for the content of this activity.)

8.2   How many movies or TV programs have you seen in
        which the action is interrupted by some well known news
        report of disaster? Eg., the famous "Day of infamy"
        broadcast in the US on Dec. 7, 1941; Neville
        Chamberlain's "peace in our time" speech in 1938. Create
        a drama around such a media event in which the action of
        the drama turns from everyday issues to the human
        reaction to news of world shaking significance. You could
        choose to invent a news event in the future for this
        activity. If you can find it, screen the short film *The
        Psychic Parrot*.

8.3   Brainstorm in a small group to list the most significant
        news stories you can remember throughout your lives.
        Attach to each story the one "signifier" that you
        remember: an image, a sound, a phrase, a gesture.
        Produce a bulletin board display explaining how the
        media sometimes summarizes an entire experience for us
        in a single "icon".

8.4   Hold a class debate on the topic: "TV news brings us real information."

8.5   Create a class list of the disasters that you have witnessed through the eyes of TV. (Earthquakes, volcanoes, famines, hurricanes, wars, assassinations.) Work in pairs to make a written record of what you know collectively about the aftermath of each of these events. Push the activity to the point of describing the actual process of receiving news. Explain why news sources do not keep us up to date on last week's stories. Invite a media professional to your class to discuss these topics and issues.

8.6   Make an inventory of all the different news sources that are available in your community. (List things like different newspapers, magazines, radio and TV stations, cable, satellite, gossip etc.) Rank and rate the sources by their importance to you, and by their reliability.

8.7   Select a single news source, and pledge to use it as your only input of news for a given period (one week minimum). Keep a journal during this exercise, to record things like:
- Iwhat you miss by being restricted to one source
- what you can and can not learn from the news source that you are assigned to
- what your exposure to this news source is teaching you about it, and about other news sources
- your evolving definition of "news"

8.8   When the experimental period is over, form small groups to compare notes on questions such as:
- do all students have the same perception about what has happened in the world during the time of the experiment? For instance, are some totally unaware of some events? Do some have different versions of events? Have they developed different beliefs about the issues and events in the news? If so, how? Why?
- what insights into the process of "witnessing" the news have you developed?
- How does your experience connect with the experiences of other students? (exchange journals)
- write a report on the experiment describing the nature of news, news reporting, news "receiving".

SCREENING IMAGES

8.9   Examine a news source over a period of time, and write a summary of the policies that seem to be in effect in the construction of this particular news source. For instance, some newspapers often have a picture of death or violence on the front page; some TV news broadcasts frequently close on a human interest story.

8.10   Make up and present a dummy of a news source consisting only of the generic descriptive information. For instance, a TV news script might go like:

"Astonishingly vivid pictures of recent world disasters in which innocent lives have been randomly lost."

"Dire predictions of impending political catastrophe from the mouth of reliable source".

"Silly pictures of political figures doing and saying unbelievably banal things at a barbecue."

"Warm family story with no news value whatsoever that tugs at the heartstrings."

THE CAMERA
ALWAYS LIES

9.1   Use some of the scenarios from the chapter, *The Camera Always Lies* as case studies for small group discussion. In each case try to determine how the media have worked to construct a version of reality that is different from actuality. Try to make recommendations in each case that would minimize the Degree of construction, or the Degree of effect on the media consumer.

9.2   Did you ever see an accident and then not recognize the write up of it in the paper? See a movie and wonder if it was the same one the reviewer saw? Attend a meeting and wonder if the one who wrote the minutes was actually there? Gather experiences of people who have witnessed an event, and then disagreed with details in its reporting. Focus on their observations of: how the reported version of the event differed from their own experience; what the report did to alter their view of the event; how much of their memory of the event relied on their experience and how much on the report. Write up these anecdotes and point out any common threads that you observe.

9.3   Go through a collection of your own family's old photographs, and make a record of your reactions and thoughts on seeing again pictures that you have not seen for many years. Produce a slide-tape show called, "Memories".

9.4   Conduct the following experiment in class over a period
        of two or three days. Be sure to emphasize the safety
        implications throughout. Construct face masks that
        restrict the wearer to a field of vision roughly equivalent
        to a movie or TV frame. You can achieve this by building
        out from a hockey or baseball mask as a base. Experiment
        with the placing of the front of the mask to discover the
        optimum distance from the eyes. It should vary between
        10 and 25 cm. Work in pairs with each mask, one as the
        wearer, and the other as the "safety", who is responsible
        to ensure that the wearer does not suffer any accident
        from the restricted vision. Exchange roles. Document the
        experiment with photographs and audio tape, or on
        video. Both students are to make a personal journal about
        their experience in each role. Spend time sharing your
        experiences in small groups, asking: "What is it like when
        your perception actually is restricted to the scope of a TV
        screen? What do you perceive? What do you miss? What
        sort of things demand your attention?" Write up a class
        report on the experiment for a local newspaper. Edit your
        pictures and tape or video into a documentary for TV or
        radio.

9.5   Select a picture from one of the sources available in the
        classroom, and paste it onto a larger piece of paper or
        card. Use a second piece of paper or card to cover the
        first, and cut a hole that registers exactly on the picture
        beneath. Now you have a peephole through which to
        view the picture you have chosen. On the original piece of
        paper or card, create more context for the picture by
        drawing details around it, or arranging other pictures in a
        way that changes the viewer's perception of the original.
        Next, move the second piece of card around in three
        dimensions, so that it allows you to see a different section
        of the first card as you move it. (Think of the camera
        moving back to reveal more of the context of a close-up
        shot.) Adapt this activity to make greeting cards,
        advertising flyers, or story books. Develop a bulletin
        board display of some of the results under the heading "
        THE CAMERA ALWAYS LIES".

9.6   Work in groups of four on the following activity. First
select a photograph from a news magazine, and post it
where the whole group can easily see it. Write the topics
"politics", "romance", "crime", "celebrity" on separate
pieces of paper, and have each group member select one
of the topics, sight unseen. Each group member's task is
to make up a news story of the type described in the draw
to accompany the picture. After working together on
drafting and revising the four news stories, the group
should display its joint work on a poster. As a follow-up
activity, conduct an inquiry into how some of the more
bizarre stories that appear in the supermarket tabloids
come to be written. You may discover that there is more
than a passing similarity between that process and the
one you have just experienced.

9.7   Using two versions of the same photograph, taken from
two copies of the same newspaper, for instance, re-
version one copy of the picture to make a different
statement from that of the original picture. You can
achieve this by masking, cropping, adding or removing
detail such as color. Mount the two versions of the
picture side by side with an accompanying text to
describe the exercise.

9.8   Screen the film *The Edit* (Prod. Mirus Films, Dist. Kinetic
Inc). Spend time in small groups discussing the ethics of
the story's events.

9.9   Have a class "talk around" in which you gather examples
of everyone's most unbelievable moments in movies.

9.10   "Second unit" films are very interesting to look at in class.
These films are often titled, *The Making of ...*, or *How We
Made ...*. They are made by second film units on the set of
a feature film to promote the feature on TV. (Or you
could screen a film on special effects, or film sound such
as *Trackstars, Hollywood FX Masters, Movie TV* or *Scanning
the Movies*.) Often these explain the great lengths film
makers go to in making what is not real appear real. A
background in a shot of ancient Rome turns out to be only
a cunningly placed painting; the squeaking footsteps in
the snow are made by a sound recordist squeezing a bag

of chamois leather. Sequences that appear to take place in the same setting were actually filmed thousands of miles apart at different times. Make up a list of precautions for viewers who do not want to be taken in by film effects.

9.11   What are the chances of these techniques being used in documentary or news programs? Do news hosts actually conduct all those interviews live each night? Could the interviews be conducted by someone else and recorded, then played back for the hosts to insert their own voices asking the same questions? When we see a host looking at a large video screen image, is that video image actually in that position? Do we read more into the relationship between them than is warranted? When we see on-air fund raising campaigns on TV, are all those phones actually busy? Or have the volunteers been instructed to pick up the phones and pretend that they are taking a pledge? If a misleading image in a fund raising campaign can be so lightly fabricated, where do we draw the line? Use these questions and concepts as the beginning of a class panel discussion or debate.

9.12   Watch a news broadcast and keep careful and detailed notes. The next day make sure that you have all the morning papers available in your community. First, work in small group with your notes from the news broadcast to develop a full description both of the news items themselves, and of their treatment in the broadcast. Then find the same news items in the newspapers. Next, join another group of students to generate a list of ideas on the difference between your perception of the news stories from TV and from the newspaper. The final product should be a list of questions either about the news stories themselves or about the treatment of them in the media. Design further activities to explore these questions.

9.13   Screen parts of feature films like *Broadcast News* or *Network*. What are the issues of television reporting that these films explore? What do they tell us about the diet of TV news that we rely on for our supply of factual information about events in the world

9.14 Screen a documentary film on the topic of the way that news is distorted in media coverage. Examples are: *The World is Watching, All the News That Fits, Consuming Hunger, Making the News Fit,* and *If It Bleeds, It Leads, Media TV or Scanning the Media.* Work in groups of four to create a lesson plan for presenting the concept of media construction to another class, using one of these films.

SIGNS, SYMBOLS
AND
ICONS

10.1   Make a collection of whole-page, color magazine ads
         with very little print in them. Paste each onto a sheet of
         clean paper, so that people can't see the back. In small
         groups examine the samples brought in by other groups
         and make notes on such things as: what kind of
         magazine you think the ad was originally in; who was
         the intended audience for the ad; what attributes of the
         advertised product are being touted; (or what associated
         attributes); how the ad tries to make sure that people
         will react to it in the expected ways; what other images
         or experiences the ad reminds us of; and how this is all
         done with images alone. Be sure always to address the
         question, "How did I know?"

10.2   Work in small groups to invent an imaginary product,
         and then create a sales campaign around it. The end
         product of the activity should be an ad that has been
         carefully constructed to appeal to a specific audience, in
         a specific market place, using specific and deliberate
         appeals. Accompanying the ad should be a
         comprehensive write-up describing the intentions of the
         campaign.

10.3   Find some media that deliberately departs from
         conventional imagery. (Eg.*Mad Magazine, Saturday Night
         Live, You Can't Do That on TV, Monty Python*) Make some
         lists of how each takes some conventional symbols or
         signs and achieves an unusual effect. (A very clear
         example, but one that is potentially sensitive for

170

classroom use, is the scene of the crucifixion in *The Life of Brian*, where all the symbolism that we have seen over and over in Biblical classics is distorted into a scene from musical comedy, not unlike the way Richard Attenborough treated World War I in *Oh! What a Lovely War*, or the way Richard Lester treated Word War II in *How I Won the War*, or the way Woody Allen or the *Monty Python* group treats almost everything.)

10.4   What modern media phenomena are popular because they depart from the conventional? Have students talk in groups about the comics, the music groups, the TV programs (*The Simpsons, Pokemon?*) that achieve popularity by first departing from the conventions, and later establishing a new convention, complete with its own sets of signs and symbols. Each group should select an example from their list for a class presentation.

10.5   What products are really hot in today's student market place? Make a class list of some such products. Sample products from the list, according to how little you are attracted to the product. (Eg. let a group of boys examine a product that is deliberately pitched at a female market; let a group of athletes examine a product that is designed to appeal to couch potatoes.) The task is to analyze the way that your particular product is marketed and represented to the target audience using signs and symbols that would be attractive to that audience. At the end of the activity, each student should make one true-confession journal entry about a new insight he or she has learnt from the exercise.

10.6   Brainstorm to list some of the common signs and symbols that exist in our society. Begin with things like "no smoking" or "no parking" signs, progress to less representational symbols such as "no entry" signs. Invent some new signs to represent such concepts as:
- this room is for mothers and children only
- beware of the dog
- lights out at 11pm.
- keep your feet off the furniture
- vegetarians only allowed
- etc., etc.

SCREENING IMAGES

10.7   Read the opening few paragraphs of a few romance novels. What do the openings have in common? How much of the commonality were you able to predict? Write an opening of your own that is typical of the ones you have read. Compare your efforts with those of two or three others. Repeat the activity with another kind of literature: Eg. detective fiction, science fiction.

10.8   Take another look at the 1938 version of *The Adventures of Robin Hood*, *Star Wars*, and *Robin Hood, the Prince of Thieves*, and *Robin Hood, Men in Tights*. Work in a group of three to write a review of the films suitable for a student newspaper. Point out all the similarities in formula and convention in the films.

10.9   Form groups of four, and assign to each group one kind of TV program. (Eg. sitcom, crime, mystery, game, soap opera) Each group is to produce a summary of the patterns, formulae and conventions that exist within its chosen genre, illustrating each point with examples from at least two shows.

10.10   Borrow or rent the film, *This is the Title of My Film*, distributed by Canadian Film Makers' Distribution Centre. After screening the film a couple of times, and discussing the way the film works, prepare a presentation of the film to another class, with the objective of illustrating the signs, conventions and patterns to be found in one popular genre.

10.11   In small groups list the kinds of films individuals like and dislike. Some, for instance will love horror films, and others will detest them. Pick one or two kinds or genres that you disagree about, and analyze each genre to list exactly what conventions, patterns, and signs you find attractive or objectionable in each genre. (Some people, for example, may be offended by some of the conventions of the fraternity house genre of film comedy.)

10.12   Take a look at advertising. What patterns, signs and conventions can you detect in the advertisements for certain kinds of products? (Eg. beer, cars, cosmetics, soft drinks, furniture)

10.13   Screen *Who Framed Roger Rabbit?*, and examine it in small groups as an example of a film that mixes the signs, patterns and conventions of the Bugs Bunny and Disney cartoon with those of the Humphrey Bogart film noir genre. (*Casablanca, The Maltese Falcon*) Describe how some other films have recently mixed the conventions of different genres, such as the *Airplane,* series, the *Top Gun* series, *L.A. Story, Wagons East.*

10.14   Watch some Hollywood Westerns. List the patterns and conventions you can find in them. Which Western films have successfully gone against the conventions? (*Butch Cassidy and the Sundance Kid*) Which ones have spoofed the conventions? (*Blazing Saddles, Wagons East*) Make a similar study of another genre. (*Dead Men Don't Wear Plaid* is an excellent study of the conventions of the film noir genre.)

10.15   Examine some of the music videos that appeal to you. What patterns do the videos use that are familiar or evocative for you? Is there any style of music video that you do not like particularly? What is it about this style that you do not like?

10.16   In recent years some new feature film genres have emerged. What are the patterns and conventions of films such as: *Nerds, Matrix,* or *Scream*? Work in groups of three to list these codes and conventions for one such film, and then write up a treatment for a new production within the same genre.

10.17   Even news programs have their own codes. How can you tell which channel you are watching from the style of the news? What are the various conventions of the different news broadcasts available in your area? Produce a news program that spoofs one of these.

GENERAL ACTIVITIES

These activities are not linked to any particular topic or theme in media education. Some are very detailed in their description of the activity, and some are less so. Some overlap with other activities. Still, in the expectation that teachers prefer to have more practical suggestions rather than fewer, I've included the whole list, despite the occasional redundancy.

11.1   Design a survey sheet to help you discover which media students have access to in their community. How many TVs in the home? Radios? Tape players? VCRs? etc. How many cinemas within fifteen minutes' drive? How many music stores? Video outlets? How many TV channels available off air? By basic cable? By pay TV? How many satellite receivers? Personal computers? Software?
Add a section which asks students to estimate the number of minutes per week they spend attending to each different medium.
Take the first draft to a test population for validation. This will tell you what you missed out, what you didn't clarify, and so on, so that you can revise and sharpen up the instrument. Design a data-base shell or a webpage for the questionnaire so that the results can be easily tabulated and reported.

Administer the questionnaire to two classes in your own school, and to two other classes at the same grade level in two different schools. Use modern technology wherever possible. (Computer networking, fax, exchange of floppy disks etc.) Write a report which details the accessibility of media to young people, accounts for variations in accessibility in different areas of your region and reports on the amount of time devoted by people to each medium. This report should be published in as public a manner as possible. A local weekly paper might be interested in helping you early in the project to give advice on making the report suitable for its pages.

As an extension activity, refine the questionnaire again in the light of your experience with its use, and apply it to classes of students of different ages in different areas, and to volunteer adults from various walks of life. Once again, aim for publication.

11.2   Take a look at how you might go about creating the conditions in which you would have to learn a lot about advertising. First you need a product, or an issue. If you have a business program in your school that uses simulations, some of the students in that program might appreciate the help of a media class in organizing their publicity. Perhaps you have a favorite charity that you'd like to boost. There could be a school event that would benefit from a publicity campaign. Or you might want to promote an issue such as recycling/conservation. Generate a list of the possibilities, and then form groups to work on the topics that take your fancy.

Find books and articles about advertising. If you can, invite a guest to the classroom who can talk from a professional point of view. Take time to talk through your campaign plans before making a presentation to the rest of the class. Make sure that each presentation includes at a minimum the following:

- objectives (very clear and realistic)

- detailed campaign plan (minimum three media: eg. poster, radio spot, direct mail, telephone campaign, telethon)
- timeline (detailed)
- budget (including outside sources)
- list of materials and equipment (including sources)
- list of responsibilities and undertakings for each group member
- detailed evaluation plan (how will you judge your own success? How will you be prepared to be judged by others?)

11.3 Working in groups of two or three, list the kinds of information you get from newspapers, and the questions you rely upon your newspaper to answer for you. Explain why people buy newspapers daily/weekly. What do people say about the newspaper on days or at times when there is none to read?

11.4 Look through a magazine with a partner. What group of readers is this magazine intended for? How can you tell? List radio stations/shows, TV, films, music that is aimed at this same audience.

11.5 Use pieces of different magazines to mock up a new magazine for a new audience. Test out your new magazine with members of that audience, and on classmates to see if they can identify the intended audience.

11.6 Invent at least 5 new TV channels, each aimed at a narrow audience, and then write a TV guide for an evening, listing program notes for each of the channels.

11.7 Put together an audio tape of a one hour radio show aimed at a narrow and specific audience.

11.8   Watch the opening two or three minutes of a TV
        drama show and fill out a chart to describe how
        much you know and how you know it about:
        • people
        • relationships
        • place
        • time
        • events
        • feelings
        • hunches/predictions
        • other comments

11.9   Talk to a partner or write in your journal about a
        time when you were forced to give up your usual
        media habits. (Eg. at camp, at the cottage, during a
        power blackout.) How did you feel at first? Later?
        What did you do instead?

11.10   As a class collect all the junk mail that comes into
        your homes over a one-week period.
        • weigh it
        • sort it into categories
        • make an audio tape of interviews about junk
          mail
        • count how many families have responded to any
          junk mail, and calculate how much they have
          spent
        • make a bulletin board display about junk mail

11.11   Organize your class to bring in a collection of old
        story books from childhood days. How many ways
        can you find to sort the collection into categories?
        What can you discover when you compare the
        collection to modern story books?

11.12   Start a class collection of buttons. Keep the buttons
        on display, constantly seeking new ways to group
        them. Invite other students to talk about your
        button collection. Keep track of the comments and
        questions they raise. How does your own
        understanding of the role of buttons in our culture
        increase as you talk to others? How are buttons like
        and unlike, stickers, T shirts and posters?

SCREENING IMAGES

11.13   Work with two other students. Each student is to watch the early evening news on a different channel. Get together to pick a news story that all channels reported, and then each is to report the story to the class, using only the information from their own particular news channel. Other class members ask questions to clarify the differences among the reports, and to bring out the amount of interpretation in news stories.

11.14   Use a stopwatch to calculate the amount/ proportion of time devoted to commercials on different channels at different times of day. Include public broadcasting channels in this survey. Present your findings on a chart. Do a similar exercise to calculate how commercials are distributed in a prime time, blockbuster movie. How long from the start of the film to the first commercial? How fast do the commercial breaks come near the end?

11.15   Make up two questionnaires, one for students and the other for adults, to survey TV viewing habits. Focus on favorite times for watching; number of hours per day watched; favorite programs and channels. Summarize the results in a written report.

11.16   Study "justice" in TV programs. Prepare an oral report on the concept of justice that you find in popular shows. (Eg. How many criminals are pursued, captured, accused, found guilty and executed without benefit of trial? How many characters justify illegal, cruel, prejudiced, biased or morally objectionable behavior on the grounds that somebody else "asked for it"? How many characters seem ready to defend the rights of the person who appears to be in the wrong?)

11.17   Brainstorm with a small group of classmates to develop a list of all the influences in your lives that shape your values and attitudes. (Eg. family, newspapers, school, friends, TV, religion, governments.) Put your list in priority order, with the most influential items at the top. Focus a class discussion on the variety of responses to this task.

11.18.   Work with some other students to create a parody of a TV program or type of program. The parody can be in the form of a video tape, a skit, a script, or a treatment, depending on the time and resources you have available.

11.19   Write letters to TV stations regularly commenting on the quality and appropriateness of their programming. Collect copies of the letters and replies into a resource binder for other media students.

11.20   Calculate the average length of each shot in TV commercials, drama programs, news programs and rock videos. Use the information to write a short comment on the costs of production of these different forms of TV programming.

GENERIC ACTIVITIES FOR MEDIA EDUCATION

12.1	Act out a simulation.
12.2	Analyze the effect of advertising upon media content.
12.3	Analyze the language/logic/rhetoric used.
12.4	Analyze for style and substance.
12.5	Arrange a co-operative education placement.
12.6	Assess the objectivity.
12.7	Brainstorm.
12.8	Calculate statistical evidence.
12.9	Check the technical aspects of the media: column inches; type face; camera angles; edits; lighting; etc.
12.10	Compare various media coverages of the same item.
12.11	Compare media coverage of an item at various times during its evolution.
12.12	Compose a bill of rights for journalists.
12.13	Compose a set of ethics for the media.
12.14	Compose a bill of rights for news consumers.
12.15	Compose and conduct a quiz.
12.16	Conduct a series of interviews.
12.17	Conduct a written debate through letters to the editor.
12.18	Contact students in another school/board/province/country.
12.19	Create your own news vehicle.
12.20	Create guidelines for a process.
12.21	Create a radio news/feature program.
12.22	Deconstruct/reconstruct.
12.23	Define.
12.24	Demonstrate the role of the news reporter as star.
12.25	Describe the role of the media.
12.26	Design a media course for another class.
12.27	Design a research project.
12.28	Determine the point of view
12.29	Develop criteria to reveal ideology in news coverage.
12.30	Do free-association writing.
12.31	Do a job-shadowing exercise with a media professional.
12.32	Edit.
12.33	Establish criteria and apply them.

12.34	Gather present knowledge and compare with level of knowledge one month later.
12.35	Improvise a docudrama.
12.36	Inspect for bias, stereotype.
12.37	Invite a speaker/guest/expert to class.
12.38	Locate on a map or in an atlas.
12.39	Make a blackboard outline.
12.40	Make up a computer simulation.
12.41	Make research notes for a biography.
12.42	Make a visit/field trip.
12.43	Make up your own activity. Negotiate it with the teacher.
12.44	Make up a test.
12.45	Make a comparison/contrast.
12.46	Make a transcript.
12.47	Make up a bibliography.
12.48	Make an anthology.
12.49	Make a factual summary, completely free of opinion.
12.50	Make a list of items and then classify the items.
12.51	Make up a time chart.
12.52	Make a clipping file.
12.53	Make a wall/bulletin board display.
12.54	Make a video/audio tape.
12.55	Make a poster.
12.56	Make a personal journal entry.
12.57	Make a multi-media display.
12.58	Make a pageant/pantomime/dumbshow
12.59	Make up a TV game show.
12.60	Make a scrapbook.
12.61	Make a chart/diagram.
12.62	Make up a board/computer game.
12.63	Make up a questionnaire/survey.
12.64	Mimic.
12.65	Mock up a newspaper/magazine layout.
12.66	Organize a seminar.
12.67	Organize a school assembly.
12.68	Paraphrase.
12.69	Parody.
12.70	Perform a consensus exercise.

SCREENING IMAGES

12.71	Perform a field-force analysis.
12.72	Précis.
12.73	Prepare research card notes for an interview.
12.74	Prepare a budget.
12.75	Present news stories in various ways to demonstrate strengths and weaknesses in news reporting.
12.76	Problematize.
12.77	Project into the future.
12.78	Replicate.
12.79	Represent as a color/animal/book title/movie/car, etc.
12.80	Research some of the history of the media.
12.81	Rewrite from another ideological point of view.
12.82	Role-play.
12.83	Satirize.
12.84	Separate fact from myth/opinion/rumor.
12.85	Set up an experiment.
12.86	Solve a moral dilemma.
12.87	Stage a formal debate.
12.88	State alternatives; assess and evaluate.
12.89	Summarize arguments on both sides.
12.90	Summarize.
12.91	Talk together to solve a problem.
12.92	Tape-record a discussion then edit it into a documentary.
12.93	Transfer into another medium.
12.94	Use a jigsaw group arrangement.
12.95	Use library resources.
12.96	Use a computer data base program.
12.97	Use electronic communications to access or report.
12.98	View alternative resources.
12.99	Work with a partner or a small group.
12.100	Write a letter to an editor/MLA/MP.
12.101	Write/make a documentary for radio/TV.
12.102	Write a ballad/song/lyric.
12.103	Write a letter to a foreign penfriend to explain.
12.104	Write a column/feature/editorial for a specific publication.
12.105	Write away for information/data/resources.
12.106	Write/perform a satirical play for stage/radio/TV.
12.107	Write a report card.

Ideas for Media Education

12.108	Write a set of rules.
12.109	Write a poem/story/script/essay/report.
12.110	Write a treatment/story-board/script for film/video.
12.111	Write a review/criticism.
12.112	Write a pamphlet/advertisement/brochure.
12.113	Write in plain language.
12.114	Write a history/survey.

APPENDIX

> # LE MORTE DE ROBIN HOOD AND HIS MERRIE ROCKETS OF THE ROUND TABLE OR HAVEN'T I SEEN YOU SOMEWHERE BEFORE, *STAR WARS*?

In the June 1978 edition of **The Ontario Film Association's** **Newsletter** **Called FRED,** *I wrote an article about the brand new film phenomenon,* **STAR WARS.** *In the year of* **TITANIC,** *it seems appropriate to revisit that article by way of a twentieth anniversary.*

  STAR WARS has just about faded away into that great film library in the sky, and I'm sorry that it did so before I had the chance to see it a couple of more times. In short, I've only seen it once. If I had seen it again, I could have made some notes about the names of the characters and settings and suchlike, making you believe I was a great film scholar, with either a photographic memory or a lot of books and periodicals to look things up in.

  What I wanted to say about *STAR WARS*, in case you're still interested, is that my sister has seen the 1938, Errol Flynn version no fewer than twelve times; and that doesn't count the number of times she's seen it on TV. After all, we know that movies on TV aren't the same as the real thing.

  If you've decided to read on anyway, I'll tell you about *STAR WARS*, and 1938, and Errol Flynn. If you were hoping to read about my sister, are reading the wrong magazine.

The 1938 version of **STAR WARS** took place in Merrie England instead of in a Galaxie (or even a Fairlane) far, far away. Both versions took place long ago. Now, in one of the versions, *THE GOOD GUYS* had a secret camp on a secret planet - how do you keep a planet secret? - and in the other *THE GOOD GUYS* had a secret camp in Sherwood Forest. In one version, *THE BAD GUYS* lived on a battle station that was so well fortified and guarded that not a single person could get inside it, or destroy it except by previous arrangement with the scriptwriter. In the other version, *THE BAD GUYS* lived in an impregnable castle, that no one could get into except by previous arrangement with the authors of the original ballad (no forwarding address available).

THE GOOD GUYS are: *THE HERO*, handsome, young, full of fealty, romantic, endowed with an uncanny accuracy in the use of weapons springing from his undoubted, unbounded and sometimes unbearable virtue. *THE HERO'S FRIENDS.* Some of these are older and wiser than *THE HERO* and seem to be there to help him out of situations that the writers decided were impossible for even him to handle on his own. The others are there for comic relief; to engage the attention of those groundlings who can't quite follow the plot and who might otherwise talk during the show. They act as foils to the intelligent, quick-witted *HERO.* One or two of these characters seem to fulfill functions that are purely mechanical. Others are there so that *THE BAD GUYS* have someone to kill, or at least shoot in the left shoulder.

Then there is the *HEROINE.* She has to be a princess. Even in galaxies far, far away, royal blood counts for something. Now everyone knows that all princesses are young, lovely, loyal and in love with *THE HERO* (sooner or later); they are in danger of being ravished by *THE BAD GUYS* (q.v.); they possess the very secret *THE BAD GUYS* need before they can afford to make mincemeat out of *THE GOOD GUYS*; they are virginal (except in the European version); brave, long-suffering, and - to everyone's amazement – capable of finding clean clothes and fresh makeup in the most unlikely and filthy places imaginable. (Sic.)

THE BAD GUYS are: *THE BOSS OF THE BADDIES.* This fella has to be the absolute epitome of rottenness, but he lacks the kind of active guts that it tales to tackle *THE HERO* head on. He is, however, the brains of the whole *BADDIE* outfit, and very much in charge. He is ruling the kingdom – or is it the galaxie? – as a(n) usurper. The rightful ruler is either dead or in some foreign prison (languishing, they call it) or both, with all his interests invested in *THE HEROINE*. (She is, after all a princess, closely related to this wronged monarch, and displaying a distinct inclination for bringing *THE HERO* very close to the throne through community property laws.)

THE HENCHMAN OF THE BOSS OF THE BADDIES. Now this one is the real nasty piece of work. Wardrobe tends to favor black for his costume, central casting yearns for the return of Raymond Massey for the part, and scriptwriters give him the kind of lines Victorian novelists would have called "dastardly". The *BADDIE* not only plans evil things the same as *THE BOSS OF THE BADDIES*, but he actually carries them out with what Italian cooks sometimes refer to as "gusto". Particularly he tends to specialize in putting *THE HEROINE* in danger of maybe having to give him a kiss, or worse.

He's in charge of the *BADDIE* armies, and comes very close to beating *THE GOODIES*, except that in the very end, virtue wins out over large numbers, and the *BADDIES* are decimated in one glorious fight that takes up most of the last reel. Excluding the final kiss and the endless credits.

There's a serious complication with *THE HENCHMAN OF THE BOSS OF THE BADDIES* as far as **STAR WARS** is concerned. The writers were not satisfied with the nastiness of *THE SHERIFF OF NOTTINGHAM* as a model. No sir. They wanted a bit of *MORGAN LE FAY*, too. Very sneaky, if you ask me. This makes it possible to make *LUKE* look like some little commoner who not only pulls the fat out of the fire, but also the sword out of the stone. Furthermore, it makes *THE HEROINE* into a more beguiling, and therefore more box-office character who takes on some of the sexual mystery of *GUENEVERE* as well as the plastic glamour of *MAID MARION*. Of course, another reason for raiding Arthurian as well as Sherwood legend is to give Sir Alec Guinness a more challenging role than *FRIAR TUCK*. That part, of course, is *MORGAN LE FAY*'s mortal enemy, *MERLIN*.

They tried to fool us with the opening rolling credits from *FLASH GORDON*. But any serious *FLASH GORDON* fan knows that half the characters in this series run around in tights and jerkins; and that *FLASH* himself affects the sword in preference to the deadly ray gun; and that the *EMPEROR MING* is only a low-budget compendium of both *KING JOHN* and the *SHERIFF OF NOTTINGHAM*.

And they tried to fool us with the music score, but that is even more 1938 than the rest of the movie. Of course there are bits that make us think of GUSTAV HOLST and his planets, and the main theme seems to have a lot in common with STRAVINSKY's PULCINELLA SUITE. When my sister first heard it, she was waiting for the bit where ERROL FLYNN swings Tarzan-like out of a tree, laughs a very merrie chuckle, and then salutes the evil SHERIFF. Did I tell you about my sister? Another time, perhaps.